I SEE YOU
B I G
GERMAN

I See You, Big German

Dirk Nowitzki and What He Means to Dallas (and Me)

Zac Crain

La
Reunion

Dallas, Texas

La Reunion Publishing, an imprint of Deep Vellum
3000 Commerce St., Dallas, Texas 75226

deepvellum.org · @deepvellum

DeepVellum is a 501c3 nonprofit literary arts organization founded in
2013 with the mission to bring the world into conversation through
literature.

978-1-64605-035-2 (paperback) | 978-1-64605-036-9 (ebook)

Support for this publication has been provided in part by
grants from the National Endowment for the Arts,
the Texas Commission on the Arts,
the City of Dallas Office of Arts and Culture's ArtsActivate program,
and the Moody Fund for the Arts:

LIBRARY OF CONGRESS CONTROL NUMBER: 2020947256

Cover design by Jeremy Biggers | jeremybiggers.com
Interior Layout and Typeset by KGT

PRINTED IN THE UNITED STATES OF AMERICA

For Isaac

I'm a dreamer
I'm this far away
You are a screamer
I hear you
This is tomorrow
And where will we stay
In a lifetime for the mavericks?

—Go Back Snowball, *"Lifetime for the Mavericks"*

Dirk,

BEFORE

I should tell you how I got here. How we got here.

The Dallas Mavericks were born six years after I was, two years after you were, and I don't remember a time when I wasn't a fan and I don't really remember ever choosing to be one. I just was. I didn't live in Dallas then, but the Mavericks were the closest team to West, Texas, the tiny town where I grew up, about an hour south.

I remember mimicking center James Donaldson's distinctive knees-up-feet-back dunks on a goal in my bedroom. The goal hung loosely on a hollow-core door, slapping hard against it whenever it was even lightly touched, so it sounded like two rocking horses fighting to the death when I did this, and I did this *all the time*, only stopping when someone banged on the other side of the door, which led to the kitchen and the rest of the house, to get me to stop. Then I'd wait a while and do it again.

The goal is no longer there, of course, but neither is the door or the house, just the memory.

I remember feeling a familial sense of pride when Mavs guard Rolando Blackman sent the 1987 All-Star Game into overtime, sinking two free throws with no time remaining, all alone on the line, shouting "Confidence, baby, con-fi-*deeeence*" as the second one fell through the

net. Ro was my favorite Maverick until you came along, even though the only jersey I owned was Mark Aguirre's No. 24. I guess it was easier for my parents to get that one for me, or maybe I was just too quiet, too shy or polite, or most likely all of that was true. (I can still be too quiet.) I wore Ro's No. 22 for my high school team, where I tried—with varying degrees of success—to replicate his smooth yet muscular jumper. So in the All-Star Game, that was our guy on the line—*my guy*—and it was a big deal, because the Mavs hadn't done much during their short time in the league. They'd go on to win the Midwest Division (RIP) that season, but that was about it.

I remember: the first time that it hurt. Do you remember the first time a game did that to you? That anything did?

I was ten years old, standing between two beds in a motel room, soaking wet, freezing cold, reeking of chlorine. The A/C unit under the window sweating like its fever just broke. I remember the confusion, watching but not seeing what was happening as Derek Harper happily dribbled out the clock against Magic Johnson and the Los Angeles Lakers in the 1984 Western Conference semifinals, the rookie point guard thinking the Mavs had won a game that was actually only tied, and *I* thought they'd won because he did. We both realized at the same time, about two seconds too late.

If they *had* won, in regulation or overtime, it would have evened the series at two games apiece, and then who knows? Maybe the momentum of an eleven-point fourth-quarter comeback would have propelled them past the Lakers and into the conference finals, and as long as we're dreaming here, maybe they would have kept going,

making it to the NBA Finals in only their fourth year of existence, going up against Larry Bird and the Boston Celtics. That's likely where it would have ended: Bird was too much for anyone to handle in 1984, the most valuable player in the regular season and the Finals.

Just getting there, though—that might have changed the trajectory of the franchise. It might have prevented everything that happened a few years later, when another disappointing loss to the Lakers, this time in the conference finals, caused the frustration that had built up by then to curdle into desperation, leading to a series of win-now decisions—trades and contract extensions, hirings and firings—that didn't even work in the short term and would spoil almost a full decade of professional basketball in Dallas, hammer-tossing what had been a model for how an expansion team should be run into an infinite pit of despair. Once there, to paraphrase the great Calexico, even their sure things fell through. The Mavericks became the kind of organization that traded away future Hall of Famer Jason Kidd after two seasons. (Jason Kidd! Two seasons! In one of which he was co-Rookie of the Year!) But maybe that would have happened anyway. And maybe that all had to happen to bring you here.

But the Mavericks didn't win against the Lakers on that night in 1984, and they didn't go on to win the series. Teams never recover from that type of disaster. The series was over exactly then. I was not old enough to understand that yet. All I knew was that it hurt, like my heart had fallen into my feet, like my body had too much blood in it. I felt stupid, foolish, the kind of emotions you really only understand the shape of much later, maybe after a few breakups. They are

certainly not something you are prepared for when you are ten years old and on vacation and the love of your life, to that point, is the cold industrial water of a motel swimming pool.

⊕ ⊕ ⊕

I grew up in West, Texas, a small town that hugs Interstate 35 like a koala does a tree, most on one side and a little bit on the other. West (despite its name) is just north of Waco, more or less in the center of the state, and its population is consistently just south of three thousand. Probably most people who live in Texas have stopped at one of the four bakeries within its city limits at some point to get a box of kolaches, the (usually) fruit-filled Czech pastries for which West is mostly known.

Have you ever stopped there?

West is also the city that made international news in 2013 when its fertilizer plant exploded, killing fifteen people, injuring around two hundred more, and destroying several hundred homes. It essentially obliterated half the town. The house I grew up in, on Reagan Street, was maybe five hundred yards away from the plant. All that's left there now, at least of what was there before, is the electrical tower the city put in our front yard, the oak tree we planted, once small enough that I could jump over the top of it and just barely brush the uppermost leaves, and the driveway. The park where I used to play basketball is gone, but a new court—donated by the Mavericks—has replaced it.

We lived on one side of the highway and my grandparents, my mother's parents, lived about a mile away on the other side. Almost always, we went to visit them instead of the other way around. They shared a big plot of land with my uncle and my great-grandmother, where my older brother and younger sister and I would throw horse apples at each other. This is also where, and I promise this is 100 percent true, I tripped over the root of a tree while playing hide-and-seek and landed on the rust-covered discarded head of a pitchfork. One of its tines punctured my ankle about an inch deep. My grandfather came out of the house, gently removed the pitchfork, and carried me inside, where he sprayed the wound with disinfectant, put a bandage on it, and sent me back outside to play. I never went to see a doctor. I was five years old.

My grandparents—we called them Leema and Papa—came over only if there was a birthday or some other special occasion. So it was a surprise to see them that evening, a Monday or Tuesday in October, just before dinner. When their car pulled in—a giant Chevy Caprice the same tawny brown as one of Leema's banana cakes, the only thing she could cook—I was at the far end of our driveway, shooting baskets on a portable hoop that always seemed about half a foot too high. What happened next was even more of a surprise: my grandfather got out of the car and came toward where I was, holding his hands out in front of him in the universal sign that he was open and ready for a pass. He had never done that before. I don't just mean call for the ball. We had never played basketball together. Never played anything, really. I loved him very much, and I know he loved

me, but he wasn't the kind of grandfather that *played*. He showed me his rock-polishing machine a couple of times, but that was it as far as recreational activities. As far as I know, that might have been the only time he held a basketball in his hands.

Not me. Starting around that time, I was always out on our makeshift court, shooting until it was too dark to see and then going by sound, sometimes rebounding a miss with my face. It was 1985. I was eleven years old and had just started junior high. I was pudgy and painfully shy and at a new school. All I did was read and play basketball and I didn't consider either to be a team sport. Maybe my parents told my grandfather all of that. Maybe he sensed it. I have no idea. My parents are too old to get a straight answer out of them now, not that I have ever fully trusted their memories, and I never asked him. I didn't have the opportunity to.

He stayed out there with me for fifteen or twenty minutes and then went inside. I was still getting up shots when he and my grandmother left, waving to me from their car before backing out. I never saw him again.

A few days later, on a sunny Friday morning, my grandfather—born Bernard F. Sulak, known to me as Papa, known to everyone else as Ben, except his wife, my grandmother, who called the man who emptied her ashtrays full of Kools and refilled her iced coffee "Beezie," short for Beelzebub, because that was her sense of humor—had a massive stroke on a sidewalk in downtown West. He was dead before they got him to the hospital.

I told my son this story the other day, about the last time I saw my

grandfather, and he reminded me that the last time he saw *his* grand-father—his mom's dad, a San Antonio Spurs fan—it also involved basketball. It was Game 3 of the 2017 NBA Finals, Golden State versus Cleveland. They watched Warriors forward Kevin Durant pull in a rebound, dribble up the court, and nail a three-pointer over LeBron James' outstretched arms to win it. A couple of months later, he suffered a heart attack at his home in Gun Barrel City.

⊕   ⊕   ⊕

I went to my first Mavs game in 1990, on a Wednesday night against the Boston Celtics, right before everything went to hell and stayed there for a long time, even a little past when you arrived.

It was a surprise. I came home and my older brother was waiting for me with his junior-college girlfriend. I don't know why. If they were trying to cheer me up, whatever it is that had happened, whatever they were trying to distract me from, I've completely blocked out, so I guess it worked.

I remember we drove to Dallas with no tickets, which is typical of my brother. He has been absurdly, almost dangerously, confident since he was born, always sure that he will be able to solve any problem, answer any question, pass any test, wriggle free from any restraint. In this case, he was correct: we bought three tickets off a scalper as we walked from the parking garage to Reunion Arena (RIP). I remember being absolutely certain that an undercover cop was going to jump out from somewhere and arrest us, right up until

we got to our seats—which were on the very top row of the upper deck—because I've never been as confident as my brother and was even less so then. I remember Larry Bird threw a behind-the-back pass for an assist about three seconds into the game. I remember Sam Perkins had a then-career-high 30 points. I remember the arena being extremely dark and the court extra bright, like we were watching a touring Broadway show instead of a basketball game.

I did not remember, until I looked it up, that the game I went to with my brother and his girlfriend happened on my dad's birthday.

It was the only game I ever saw at Reunion Arena, which has been gone so long that I don't even recall when it was torn down, though I have a dim memory, a screenshot of a since-deleted clip in my mind, of driving past it when it was mostly demolished and only the flat oval roof remained, along with a bare structure holding it aloft, and so it looked like a faux-modern coffee table, the kind that hemorrhages style and quality the longer you look at it, meant for a glance and nothing more. It feels impossible that you ever played there, and yet you did—for two full seasons. It sometimes feels like you were always on the Mavericks.

While we were at the game, it did not feel like I was witnessing the last gasps of the team I had grown up loving. It didn't feel like that at any point that season, really. Joan Didion wrote, "It's easy to see the beginnings of things, and harder to see the ends." I was a sophomore in high school, and I thought the world would never end and I also thought I wouldn't live past the age of twenty-six, so what did I know about endings? Or anything? The Mavs finished 47–35 in

1990, bouncing back from only thirty-eight wins the previous season, and it looked like that had been a fluke, just a blip on an otherwise upward path. But it wasn't an aberration. It was a harbinger of
things to come, a stutter step before the fall, before the franchise tumbled o

v

e

r

t

h

e

e

d

g

e

o

f

a

cliff.

Before:

THE NEAR DEATH OF PROFESSIONAL BASKETBALL IN DALLAS, TEXAS

(not to be too dramatic about it)

(but it was dramatic)

In 1990–91, Roy Tarpley—the troubled big man the team had built itself around, while he himself was precariously balanced on a massive substance abuse problem—played just five games, the last five he would play until 1994–95, due to multiple violations of league policy. (Tarpley played fifty-five games before being suspended again, this time permanently. He died in 2015, only fifty years old.) The Mavs might have been able to withstand his absence if the rest of their roster wasn't seemingly assembled by someone who had just woken from a four-year coma. Alex English left his Hall of Fame career behind in Denver; in Dallas, the thirty-seven-year-old forward was so washed he was stonewashed. He was relaxed-fit-dad-jeans Alex English. Fat Lever, a former All-Star, played only four games and was never the same do-everything guard the team thought it had acquired. Blackman and Harper were still around, but they weren't nearly enough, and they were getting older, too.

They won only twenty-eight games and it was still somehow one of the team's best seasons of the 1990s, a decade in which they

won more than thirty games only one other time and endured back-to-back seasons of eleven and thirteen wins.

The 1990s were a terrible time for the Mavs to be terrible. Dallas is a football town even when the Cowboys are a slow-motion disaster. But then they were good again, winning Super Bowls in 1992, 1993, and 1995 and remaining contenders for the rest of the decade. The Texas Rangers were also suddenly relevant, opening a new stadium in 1994 and winning division titles in 1996, 1998, and 1999. And the Mavericks were sharing Reunion Arena with the Dallas Stars, who relocated from Minnesota in 1993 and were led by Mike Modano, a handsome center who happened to be arguably the best American-born hockey player in the history of the game, a Hall of Famer just entering his prime, who would lead the team to a Stanley Cup in 1999. Even the new Major League Soccer franchise—then known as the Dallas Burn—was successful, winning the U.S. Open Cup in 1997 and making the playoffs in its first seven seasons, and doing it in the heart of Dallas, at the Cotton Bowl.[1] The Mavericks were lagging behind everyone. Maybe even a few high school teams.

It wasn't just sports. Dallas was on the way up, or at least it wanted to be.

When I moved to Dallas for good in March 1998, the downtown area was mostly dead and the parts that weren't were dying.

---

1. They would eventually change their name to FC Dallas, just before leaving Dallas and the Cotton Bowl for a soccer-specific stadium in Frisco, a suburb thirty miles north.

It felt like the pie-shaped building where I worked on the edge of downtown—which had formerly housed the radio station KLIF, where the the Top 40 format was born—was hanging off a clearance rack, like the area had already been picked over and what was left was past its expiration date or not good enough to begin with. It certainly didn't feel like it was on the verge of a comeback. Even Didion probably couldn't have seen a beginning there.

There were two bond elections held in 1998 that aimed to change that. One of them, in terms of the scope of the ambition it was attached to, seemed the more obvious bet to change the course of Dallas's future and had much more support. The Trinity River Project had many components, but the main one, the one that sold the whole thing, was the creation of what the carnival barkers behind it would often call the biggest urban park in the country.

More than two decades later, it still doesn't exist. Maybe because you weren't involved.

I'm only partly joking, because the other bond election—much more contentious, and passed by only around 1,600 votes—was to build the arena that came to be called the American Airlines Center. It's not a stretch to say you made that deal a success. (Fittingly, the city council voted to retire the last $10 million or so of remaining bonds, paying off the last of the debt from the AAC, on June 22, 2011, seventeen years ahead of schedule and just over a week after you led the Mavericks to an NBA title.) The city council should have named the street outside the arena Nowitzki Way—which they did, in 2019—for that reason alone.

But the city didn't rename that stretch of Olive Street because of a real estate deal, even one that was instrumental in rescuing a part of the city that had been an EPA brownfield site. And the city council didn't vote unanimously to change the name solely because of what you did at the AAC. It's because of *how* you did it all, and how long: the loyalty and love you showed us for two decades and counting, how you became a model Dallas Maverick and a model Dallasite.

"My first year, the city wouldn't have named a dumpster after me, much less a street," you joked, when the new name was made official at a ceremony at the arena on October 28, 2019. Never taking yourself too seriously—that was the Nowitzki way, too.

⊕ ⊕ ⊕

By the time I moved to Dallas, the Mavericks were mostly off my radar, if I'm being completely honest. I had been in Austin, finishing college, and if the team could barely turn heads at home, three hours down I-35 their presence was nonexistent. After a few years, it was almost as though I had made them up, or maybe they had moved to a different city and changed their name, like the old Dallas Chaparrals of the ABA had become the San Antonio Spurs.

After coming home to West in the summers, I would leave for Austin not long before training camp started, hoping as ever that *this* would be the season where it would start to turn around, not dreaming of a playoffs spot, just a clear sightline to respectability. By the time I would come back home for Thanksgiving break and finally

get a chance to check in and catch up, the season was already lost, not worth the effort it would take to stay in touch. (This was largely pre-internet.)

In a way, I was better off. I didn't really have to suffer all that much during the Mavericks' decade in the desert. It mostly passed by like a movie montage, years and years and years of gruesome futility flickering by while the piano part from "Layla" plays. I was spared the full weight of it. But I slowly became disconnected from the team, too. I know I wasn't alone, but I still feel guilty about it. I didn't intend to abandon the Mavs when they were at their lowest, I promise. It just happened that way. I didn't keep in touch with a lot of my other high school friends, either.

And that's why it took me and everyone else a few years before we trusted you, why we all heard the name "Dirk Nowitzki" and only thought we were getting more of the same. Why I never could have predicted that you would be a constant presence in my life for the next two decades, longer than any relationship in my life that doesn't involve blood, outliving the entirety of a marriage, a couple of jobs, a cat, a few dogs, and I don't know how many cars. I don't know a life in Dallas without you in it.

I guess at some point I started to think you'd always be here.

1

A Pessimist Comes to America

"That game was the biggest thing in my life," you'd say later.

March 28, 1998, was your grand opening, your official introduction to the basketball world. The USA Basketball Junior National Select Team was facing off against a squad of players from around the world at the (somewhat confusingly named) Alamo Stadium Gymnasium in San Antonio. The fourth annual Nike Hoop Summit was meant to be a showcase for high schoolers Al Harrington and Rashard Lewis, both expected to skip college and jump straight to the NBA. And the two American players held up their end, Harrington scoring twenty-six points (the most by a homegrown player at the Hoop Summit to that point) and Lewis adding eighteen and a record four steals.

But they were overshadowed by a lanky kid with floppy hair and broad shoulders and a name no one could seem to pronounce or even spell correctly—several times on the ESPN broadcast it appeared as "Nowitzki." You were only nineteen years old then and had snuck out of Germany to be there, with your club team, the Würzburg X-Rays, on the verge of promotion from the second

division in the Basketball Bundesliga. You had almost backed out of the trip for that reason; you didn't want to disappoint anyone. But you hadn't worked all that time just to play against the top teams in Germany. Whose goal was that? You had to go to America. "This is where my future is," you said.

Your answer gained a bit of confidence when it was relayed to viewers by play-by-play announcer Dan Shulman. The truth was, you didn't know how good you were, and that was why you went—to see. It was a chance, your only one, really, to go up against high-level competition, players your age who were actually trying, and measure how you stacked up.

You were in the third year of a five-year plan, so it was a good time to benchmark your progress. Your coach and mentor (and second father and agent and best friend), Holger Geschwindner, had told you at the beginning, three weeks after you started working together, "If you want to be the best player in Germany, we can stop practicing right now. If you want to be with the best guys in the world, we have to practice every day. It's a major decision, but you have to make it." To show your commitment, you got your driver's license and convinced your parents to buy you a white Volkswagen Rabbit so you could drive an hour each way from Würzburg to train with Holger at the Abtenberghalle in Rattelsdorf. (The Abtenberghalle's name makes it sound much grander than what it was, as you know: a tiny gym with a corrugated metal roof and industrial white paint job. It was a shed with a hardwood floor.)

Your parents had already given you much more than a car and

the encouragement to pursue your dream. Your mother, the former Helga Bredenbröcker, was a member of the team that represented West Germany at EuroBasket Women 1966 in Romania. "A bankshot specialist" is how she would describe her game later. Your father, Jörg-Werner, played handball for the country's national team; basketball wasn't thought of as a sport for a man, or at least Jörg-Werner didn't think of it that way, or at least he didn't then. The product of those two sets of genes—Helga is five foot ten, Jörg-Werner around six foot one—you were probably destined for some level of athletic achievement.

Your first sport was tennis. Like many Germans, Helga and Jörg-Werner had picked up rackets following the Grand Slam successes of Steffi Graf and Boris Becker. You started playing with your parents when you were young, before you were even in grade school, and rose to become a nationally ranked player on the junior circuit. Eventually, though, you grew too tall for the game, twice the height of some of your opponents. By then, you were more interested in basketball, anyway, after seeing the U.S. Men's National Team, a.k.a. the "Dream Team," at the 1992 Barcelona Olympics.

You started hanging around where the X-Rays played when you were fourteen. That's where a youth coach noticed you, saw your height and the way you moved, and said you could be the next Toni Kukoč, the Croatian star who would soon go on to play with Michael Jordan and the Chicago Bulls during their second trio of championships. But the possibility of that happening seemed unlikely—the history of German players in the NBA could fit on a book jacket.

There was Detlef Schrempf, who was well-known enough to later play himself on *Parks & Recreation* and have a really good Band of Horses song named after him. He made the All-NBA third team in 1995, three All-Star games, and was the Sixth Man of the Year twice. But who else was there? The idea of playing in the same league as Jordan and his Dream Team teammates—or, like Kukoč, on the same team—was less a fantasy than a delusion. So you were tall. So what?

It didn't help that, though you had inherited your athleticism from both sides, when it came to temperament, you were much more like your mother (a pessimist) than your father (the eternal optimist). But you kept playing, kept growing, and that brought you to the attention of Holger. He was in his late forties then, but still competitive, six foot four and in shape, playing on a senior team. He first saw you while waiting for a game in Schweinfurt and was struck by a "tall, skinny kid running around the court," raw and unpolished but practically vibrating with potential.

"He did a lot of things right," Holger told me in 2009, "what a good basketball player is able to do, but he had no technical skills. No shooting. No dribbling. But you could see that the guy had a sense for the game. We shared the same locker room, so I said, 'Hey, who is teaching you the tools?' And he said, 'Nobody.' So I said, 'If you want, we can do it.'

"Three weeks later, we played a game in Würzburg. He and his parents and his sister were there. After the game, Helga came over and said, 'Hey, Dirk told us you offered to practice with him. Can we do that?' So we started the next day."

Holger, the former captain of the West German team at the 1972 Munich Olympics, had unorthodox methods for building you into the best possible basketball player he could. Do they still seem as strange as they did then? He taught you precise shooting mechanics—around that time, in 1995, he believed he had discovered the optimal angle for releasing a jumpshot, sixty degrees—but he also had you rowing, skating (on ice and off), playing tennis, fencing, doing calisthenics, and learning to play the saxophone. Among other things.

"The main problem," Holger told me, "was I had never been educated in teaching like this in sports. I loved the sport and I played first division until I was fortysomething. But I wanted to find out whether I'm able to transport all that knowledge to kids. He was playing for the youth team, in the second division, so nobody was really watching what was going on. We stayed to our program. We had a pretty theoretical approach. We didn't have to look what the other guys were doing."

It was unusual but effective. In one tournament, you led a select team of kids from Würzburg against the Netherlands' U-22 national team, and you scored your side's first twenty-eight points. "The opponents always knew what was coming but could not prevent it," your team's coach, Klaus Perneker, recalled a few years ago in an interview with *Vice*. (The Würzburg kids won the game and took first place overall.) After you had a good game in France for Germany's U-18 team, American college coaches started calling your house. By September 1997, you were already enough of a known quantity—perhaps the best

player in Germany, certainly the best young player in the country—that you were picked for a team that would play a couple of exhibition games against a traveling squad of NBA players, led by Charles Barkley and Scottie Pippen, under the banner of Nike NBA Hoop Heroes. What had seemed so far off was suddenly RIGHT THERE.

Barkley, whose play with the Dream Team inspired you to wear No. 14 (which you later transposed to 41 when you joined the Mavericks and guard Robert Pack wouldn't give it up), and Pippen, whose poster was on your wall—two actual Dream Teamers, teammates of Jordan, NBA superstars, future Hall of Famers. There were others—Jason Kidd, Reggie Miller, Vin Baker, coming off his first All-NBA team and already a three-time All-Star—but those two were enough. Just being on the court with them was enough.

And it couldn't have gone any better. The games were just exhibitions, but they showed you that maybe it was possible. They weren't *letting* you score all those points. Maybe a few business decisions were being made—it was September in Berlin and there were no names on the front of the jerseys, just Nike swooshes—but pride wouldn't allow these guys, these grown-ass men, to let an eighteen-year-old kid with a buzz cut score at will on them. And you were doing it anyway. The clips on YouTube show you skinnier and bouncier and wearing No. 78, but your silhouette cuts through the decades, your jumper identical, the results the same.

How many times have you heard Barkley talk about that game? He changes the story a bit the more he tells it—and he's told it plenty—but he's remained pretty consistent on the amount you scored during

one of those games. ("Dirk scored a smooth fifty points," he told me in 2009; a decade later, he'd upped it to fifty-two.) "He was too big for Scottie Pippen and, I forget, we had another really good defender —I can't remember who it was at the time—and he just whooped their ass." After the game, he approached you and said that however much money it would cost to convince you to go to Auburn, his alma mater, he would pay it himself.

At the time, you *were* considering coming to the United States to attend college for a year or two. Three dozen universities had officially registered their interest, and those were just the ones that thought they had a shot at getting you on their campus. There were two front-runners. Ben Braun had been chasing you pretty much since the moment he took the head coaching job at Cal. Kentucky wanted you, too. You would have helped the Wildcats defend the title they won in San Antonio, the day after your appearance at the Hoop Summit.

But the Hoop Summit proved—maybe not to you yet, maybe not to Holger or your parents, but absolutely to everyone else—that there wasn't much you could learn in college, at least not on the court.

⊕   ⊕   ⊕

Remember what Holger told you before that game in San Antonio?

He said: Every time you get the ball, take it to the rim and try to dunk it. And if they knock you down, do it again. And again. "They cannot get the courage out of you."

It was 10–4 and the World team could barely get the ball over the half-court line, much less get into anything resembling an offense. Finally, you got the ball on the right wing and caught your defender, Jason Capel, leaning the wrong way. You took it hard to the lane with your left hand; you always liked doing that. JaRon Rush—who would go on to play at UCLA but is probably better known as the older brother of future NBA players Kareem and Brandon—got there too late to do anything other than foul you as you attempted a two-handed dunk, just like Holger said.

As you went to the line, your stats for the X-Rays flashed on the screen: *30.0 points, 16.0 rebounds, 9.0 assists.* They were so outrageous they felt made up—I know Germans are efficient, but not to the point of perfectly divisible statistics—and maybe they were. You don't have to tell me. I will say that the assists number especially seemed like wishful thinking on someone's part.

But as the game wore on, it was clear that if the numbers on the screen were just something that you or Holger wrote down before the game, a guesstimate for the ESPN broadcast crew, they were representative of what you were capable of at just nineteen years old. Just like in the exhibitions against the Nike barnstorming team in Berlin, the version of you we all know is easily recognizable in this game, the strange number (you wore 15 in San Antonio) the only detail that would give anyone pause. You ended up with thirty-three points and fourteen rebounds, the former a record that lasted until 2010 when Enes Kanter scored thirty-four. A handful of U.S. players fouled out trying to stop your repeated forays to the hoop. You looked like the

player a Cal assistant would compare to Pippen: "He's long, lean, and he's got the first step."

It was just one game, but it was enough. "If you went by that tape alone," Larry Bird told *Sports Illustrated*, "you'd think he's one of the best ever."

(I will admit that I did not see the game until years later, not until you were well on the way to making Bird's words a reality. I had just gotten to Dallas then, a few weeks earlier. The night after the Hoop Summit, I went to see Radiohead and Spiritualized perform at the Music Hall at Fair Park, which normally hosts touring musicals—my parents took me and my sister to see them when we were kids—so it was an appropriately theatrical venue. Radiohead was on their *OK Computer* tour, and it was arguably the best possible time to see them, as their ambition was leading them to redefine what rock music could be, but they were still beholden to at least some of its conventions. You could see where they were headed ("Nude," which would show up on 2007's *In Rainbows*, made its full-band debut at that show) but they weren't there yet. As far as scouting went, I was much more interested, at the time, in what the future looked like for Thom Yorke and company rather than for the Mavericks, who were finishing up a decade of letting me and everyone else in Dallas down. And if you went by that concert alone, you'd think they were one of the best ever. Anyway.)

The Hoop Summit changed everything for you. Before, it had been a discussion about whether the next level for you was playing at an American college or for a European team. After San Antonio,

there was a third option, even if you downplayed the possibility: jumping straight to the NBA.

You and your coaches insisted you weren't ready, that you weren't strong enough or good enough, that you needed a year in Europe, maybe two, before it was time for the NBA. Maybe a year in college and then another at Benetton Treviso or Barcelona. At least this is what you told everyone publicly. But I know you and Holger had begun to think the idea wasn't so crazy. If it was the right situation, where you could grow into the game, play and develop and learn on the job, why wait? You ultimately wanted to be in the NBA, so why not start figuring out the game right then? But you would have to be strong to do it. On the court, you were ready. Off the court, Holger still needed to find out. He had to test you.

The two of you had come to America briefly in December on Christmas vacation. In May, you came back for your official visits to Kentucky and Cal. While here, you and Holger decided to visit the Grand Canyon. After arriving at the base camp on the south side, Holger told you that the next morning you'd take the South Kaibab Trail down from the South Rim to Phantom Ranch and the Indian Garden and back up to the top, seven miles and an elevation change of almost five thousand feet one way, via an endless series of switchbacks.

He had done it a few times before and knew it was more taxing mentally than physically. "I wanted to see, you know, how he's reacting, seeing all those lanes—another one, and another one, and another one, and on and on and on. He did a great job, so I was pretty sure we could handle all the challenges ahead of us."

Cal and Kentucky both offered you scholarships, and you've said (and Holger has said) that you probably would have picked Cal if you had decided to play collegiately. But that idea had been more or less abandoned before you even got back to Germany from the U.S. trip.

That weekend, after your visits to both schools, you entered your name into the NBA draft.

You and Holger have both insisted that you didn't think you'd be taken very high, that maybe you would even slip into the second round. Occasionally you have even suggested that you thought you might not have been drafted at all. Which is ridiculous now, knowing everything that happened, but it was also ridiculous then. Jerry West—the literal NBA logo, who would be in the Hall of Fame even if he had never played for the Lakers, just for his acumen as an executive and as a George Lucas-level worldbuilder—thought you were the second-best player in the draft. Not a decade later, when it was no risk to say such a thing. *Then*, in 1998. And Rick Pitino was desperate to draft you and even arranged to meet you in Rome, and can you imagine if that had happened? Dealing with Larry Bird comparisons because you were white and tall and looked like you might know your way around a tractor while playing where the actual Larry Bird had played, and being coached by Pitino, who was burning through players like he was in career mode in *NBA2K*, and standing at the center of a media spotlight that was so hot and bright it made sunshine feel like shade, where you'd essentially be in a press conference every waking hour? You might have gone home before your first season was over. It was hard enough in Dallas.

Reading back over what Holger said at the time, it's more likely that he was just trying to exert some control over the situation, which led to some fantastic quotes. "It's probably looking like he'll stay in Europe because the Olympics are coming up and the national team wants him," he said on June 15 with the draft approaching. "Right now, he's a kid who still likes roller skating and stuff. I guess it doesn't make too much sense right now to send him away from home."

And the next day, after you officially declined the offers from Cal and Kentucky and Holger said you were going to withdraw your name from the draft, too: "Of course, his basic idea is to one day play in the NBA. But if you start too soon, then you're sitting on the bench. He's not a guy who needs to learn how to fly around the United States to sit on different benches."

⊕   ⊕   ⊕

Were you trying to get to Dallas? Did you know, did Holger know, that's exactly where you needed to be? The city, the team, the coach—it was all just right. Dallas was big but not too big. The Mavericks were bad, maybe even terrible, but they'd at least stopped getting worse. And Don Nelson was the kind of offensive mind who knew just what to do with a seven-foot kid with an instructional-video jumper. Nellie had invented the point forward with Paul Pressey in Milwaukee and discovered the future of basketball with the Run TMC teams at Golden State.

But even if this was what you wanted, you couldn't have known the Mavs would go out and get you a best friend, too.

"Things could not have gone better," Don Nelson crowed after the June 24 draft. "Everything we wanted to accomplish, we did. That doesn't happen much in life."

According to your buddy Marc Stein, the former Mavs beat reporter for *The Dallas Morning News*, Mavs owner Ross Perot Jr. told Nelson he had to have two picks in the first round if he wanted to use one on you, "to ensure that Dallas's long-suffering fans would have someone to root for" in the next season. And very briefly—partly thanks to you, in fact—the Mavs did have a second first-round pick. Before the draft, Nelson made a deal with the Milwaukee Bucks, who were picking ninth and wanted Robert "Tractor" Traylor, an All-American big man from Michigan built like a Cajun chef. Nelson agreed to pick Traylor at No. 6, as long as you were available for the Bucks to take at No. 9. If so, then Milwaukee would trade you and its other first-round pick (No. 19) to the Mavs in exchange for Traylor.

It was a calculated risk. Nelson had tried to hide you from other teams, as much as he could, and downplayed his interest in the big kid from Germany. It worked. He wanted you all along and he got you, but he had head-faked the Bucks into giving up another asset in the process (and maybe tricked Pitino and the Celtics into not trading up for you). He used the extra pick he got from Milwaukee to make a deal for Steve Nash, then the third-string point guard in Phoenix. "Things could not have gone better" ended up being an

understatement, since it was the first time in NBA history that two future MVPs were acquired on the same day.

(The Mavericks would, somewhat unbelievably, do this again twenty years later, almost to the day, making a franchise-altering, draft-night deal that would bring another nineteen-year-old European basketball genius to Dallas: Luka Dončić. This time, it was a bit like they traded for you and Steve again, but stuffed into one player. Like Mark Twain said, "History doesn't repeat itself, but it often rhymes.")

There was another risk for Nelson and the Mavs. Holger was still saying you wouldn't be in the NBA "before the year 2000," as he put it to Stein, that you intended to play for Germany at the 2000 Sydney Olympics and then come over. A handful of teams in Italy, Spain, and Greece were prepared to sign you to a (tax-free) $2 million-a-year contract in the interim; the Mavs could only offer $1.3 million. But the Nelsons, Don and his son Donnie, at least got you and Holger to hold off on signing anything until they could come to Germany and meet with you. They got on a plane the afternoon after the draft, planning to meet Perot, who was already in Europe on business. Nelson joked that he would just stay on your family's porch until he could convince you to come back home with them. His real pitch, according to the Fort Worth *Star-Telegram*: "I'll sell him on the fact that he's an up-and-coming young player joining an up-and-coming young team, that the fit is right, that he'll get great coaching as opposed to playing in a lesser league. And that we have a great state and a great city. I know he likes what he knows of it."

You did know a little bit. You'd stopped in Dallas for a training

camp with the World team before heading to San Antonio for the Hoop Summit game. And you knew a little about the Nelsons, too. Donnie was an assistant coach for the World team and had arranged for them to play at the downtown YMCA. He first met you and Holger in the lobby of the Hyatt next to Reunion Tower, when he was sent to pick you up.

The World team had a few players who would go on to play in the NBA—most notably Luis Scola, Dan Gadzuric, and Darius Songaila— so you had to take the workouts at the Y seriously, to ensure that you were not only on the roster but a starter. Otherwise, what was the point of coming all this way? The Nelsons, then, got a rare chance to see everything you were capable of, up close, while everyone else was working off a no-definition videotape, if that, and European video-tapes were notorious for promising Sasquatches that turned out to be bears with mange. They could see how fluid you were, how easily you handled the ball, the footwork, and that jumpshot, so perfect and pic-turesque it was like you were shooting from the base of a trophy.

Nelson the elder later told ESPN's Tim MacMahon: "Word eventually got out on him, but we still knew more about him than anybody in the draft."

Off the court, you got to see more of Dallas than any other U.S. city. It wasn't what a guidebook would recommend—observation deck at Reunion Tower, sure; Dealey Plaza, OK; Medieval Times, *eh*—but it was enough to get comfortable, to be able to imagine your-self not just in an NBA city but this specific one. Now you wouldn't have to imagine it.

You got an exemption from the German Basketball Federation to stay home while the U-22 team traveled to a tournament in Spain. Perot and the Nelsons took you and your family out to dinner as soon as they arrived in Würzburg. The idea of you going to the United States to play basketball wasn't unfamiliar to your parents. Their daughter, Silke, five foot ten and four years older than you, had done it, averaging four points and two rebounds as a walk-on freshman at Duquesne University in Pittsburgh in 1993–94. She played well enough to earn a scholarship in her second semester. But she only lasted nine months in America. She was desperately homesick, calling her mother over Christmas in tears.

"I'd say Dirk has to be prepared that it's not going to be easy," Silke told Marc Stein. "He has to be strong at the beginning. There is a language problem, and the culture shock is strong, but if you go there with the feeling that it's not going to be easy, I think he will be fine. The whole year meant a lot to me as a person, being all by myself. I learned to deal with problems." She wanted you to go. So did your father, who bonded with Nellie, your potential coach, over beers. He told you to "seize the opportunity."

"This has hit us like a typhoon," Jörg-Werner said, after you and Holger flew back to Dallas with the Nelsons to continue the courtship. Four days after being drafted, you landed at DFW Airport and were nailing jumpers in front of a group of reporters immediately after a ten-hour flight.

In your luggage, you had brought your own towel, just in case.

It would have been overwhelming to anyone, being at the center

of this typhoon that had now made land in Dallas. After you arrived, the Nelsons brought you to the team's practice facility for a private workout. Then they packed a week into the next day. They took you to Thurgood Marshall Recreation Center in South Dallas, where sixty or so kids chanted your name. They took you to the site where the American Airlines Center would be built and showed you the plans. Perot made the Nelsons buy you a suit, your first. ("I live in Würzburg—what do I need a suit for?" you said.) You wore the suit to a press conference at Reunion Arena, where you were introduced with Nash, resulting in an absolutely iconic image. Nash is on Nellie's left, a bleach-blond dye job growing out, looking like the Mavs had traded for the trumpet player in a ska-punk band. You are on Nellie's right, a perfunctory quarter smile on your face, looking impossibly German, like you'd just been sent to kill Bruce Willis at Nakatomi Plaza, with floppy Backstreet Boys hair, hanging-with-Derek-Zool-ander gold hoop earrings. It's an incredibly 1998 photo.

The day ended with a cookout at Nellie's house with a few play-ers in attendance. Michael Finley and Nash were there, and Shawn Bradley and Samaki Walker. "That was pretty much the situation when we had to make the decision," Holger told me, "sitting on Don Nelson's pool all night long and saying, *To do or not?*"

The Nelsons and Perot wanted an answer from you before you flew back to Germany the next day. It was a Tuesday and the NBA lockout would start at midnight. They wouldn't be able to talk to you again until it was over. The time spent with the Nelsons had won over Holger. Your mom was the only holdout; she was being

protective. But she called you Tuesday morning and gave her bless-
ing, so you put on your new/only suit again and met reporters again,
now officially a Dallas Maverick, or as close as you could get.

You said that an impromptu game of one-on-one with Walker,
the team's six-foot-eight power forward, at Nelson's cookout had
sealed the decision for you. "I think my offense is pretty good. I can
compete with them," you said at the press conference. "Defense, I
have to work hard, learn a bit more. I hope it works out."

Then you flew back to Germany.

⊕   ⊕   ⊕

Like I said, I moved to Dallas in March 1998, a couple of weeks before
you came to Texas for the first time for the Nike Hoop Summit. You
would join me full-time at the beginning of 1999. It's safe to say that
neither one of us knew what the fuck we were doing here for a while.

Back then: Bill Clinton was still president of the United States.
George W. Bush was governor of Texas, just starting to consider a run
for the White House. Michael Jordan had just played his final game
as a Chicago Bull, after hitting the game- and series-winning shot in
Game 6 of the NBA Finals against the Utah Jazz, ending the fabled
"Last Dance." The day after you were taken with the No. 9 pick at
General Motors Place in Vancouver, Microsoft released Windows
98. A few months later, on September 4, Stanford Ph.D. candidates
Larry Page and Sergey Brin founded Google in Menlo Park.

In Dallas: on May 2, voters approved a $543-million bond to

fund eleven capital improvements, the most notable of which was the Trinity Corridor Project; as I mentioned, the park promised as part of that concern has not, as of December 2020, opened. Construction has not yet begun. It probably won't get started until Max or Morris Nowitzki wins his own NBA title. At the same time, Mayor Ron Kirk was pushing for the redevelopment of a brownfield on the edge of downtown, the former home of the Dallas Electric Company generating plant. The key to Kirk's plan was a new multisport arena, which would replace Reunion Arena as home of the Mavericks and Stars.

Me: I wasn't watching much basketball in 1998, or at least I wasn't watching much of the Mavericks. They were awful and had been awful. They won just twenty games in 1997–98 and that was after starting the season 3–0. Jim Cleamons, who was supposed to bring the Bulls' championship ways with him from Phil Jackson's coaching staff, was fired sixteen games into his second season, after winning a total of twenty-eight games. Nellie, who had been general manager, replaced him, and ended up supervising a fifteen-game losing streak. The only highlight of the season was A. C. Green breaking Randy Smith's consecutive games played record (906). They did not qualify for the playoffs.

I was too busy to watch, anyway. I was twenty-four and working as the music editor at the *Dallas Observer*, the city's then-thriving alternative weekly newspaper (we had fourteen staff writers and every issue was two hundred pages; now it's more like one writer and forty pages, on a good week). I was living in an apartment off Greenville Avenue that had a hot water leak in the shower that the

management refused to fix and so it maintained 100 percent humidity 100 percent of the time. It was like I was living in a greenhouse. When I eventually moved out, I discovered that the posters I had on the wall had been steamed in place, as though a street team had wheat-pasted them there. It was the kind of small-world apartment complex that only exists in a TV series—one of my neighbors was an arts writer for the *Dallas Morning News* and another played guitar in a popular local band. In the latter's unit, every flat space above the floor was covered with empty beer cans or whiskey bottles.

It wasn't the best time to be living in Dallas. Prior to moving there, I had only seen the city at its finest, enhanced by the glow of special occasions. In the spring, my parents and my sister and I came for Easter weekend, spending the night at the hotel attached to the Galleria mall, with its ground-floor ice rink; in the summer, we came for the musicals at Fair Park in the Spanish Baroque-style Music Hall; in the winter, it was Christmas shopping at the sleek and modern NorthPark Center Mall, surrounded by developer Raymond Nasher's art collection. We would pass downtown on the way, and the gleaming skyline distracted me from looking closer. If I had, I would have realized that the core of the city was crumbling. Downtown had been overbuilt during the "Perpetual Boomtown" years of the 1970s and early 1980s. When an economic depression came in the mid-eighties, it made the bottom seem so much further down. By the end of the nineties, it was gray and shabby and empty, sapped of the can-do energy that had rescued the city in the 1960s. As my late boss, Wick Allison, put it, arguing in favor of building

a new arena in *D Magazine* in January 1998, "Measured against almost every other major city, our downtown is a wasteland." In the previous decade and a half, he noted, it had lost nearly $1 billion in tax revenue. There were glimmers of a comeback—the promise of a new arena, Nasher moving the bulk of his renowned collection to a sculpture garden he planned to build—but nothing had taken root yet.

But if it was a bad time to be living in Dallas, it was a great time to be the music editor of the city's alt-weekly newspaper. The *Observer* building was on the edge of Deep Ellum, home to the city's music scene going back to the 1920s, when blues musicians like Robert Johnson, Lead Belly, and Blind Lemon Jefferson played there. It had gone through regular booms and busts in the decades since, and, when I got to Dallas, it was coasting along at the end of its latest renaissance, brought on by alternative rock bands like Toadies and Tripping Daisy. In a few years, people would decide that the area was too dangerous, which was more reputation than actual fact and brought on by the presence of hip-hop and dance clubs and their largely Black clientele. It was ridiculous. But in 1998, Deep Ellum was still flourishing. There was Club Clearview (which had gotten its start with a group of friends, including future Mavericks owner Mark Cuban, throwing outlaw warehouse parties), Trees (so named for the sightline-blocking poles inside), Curtain Club, Galaxy Club, and a few others. I wasn't cool, but in Deep Ellum I could pretend that I was. I got into any show that I wanted and got free drinks once inside, from either the band or one of the bartenders or someone I met there.

When I was starting out at the *Observer*, I lived in that apartment off Greenville Avenue for a year and a half and it was kind of a lost year and a half, an eighteen-month jumble of bourbon and Marlboro Lights. (My timing was a little off: about a year later, the Granada Theater would reopen as a live music venue about a block away. But maybe that was for the best.) I'd like to think that my life then was some mix of *Almost Famous* and *High Fidelity*, and maybe it was, if you edited the highlights together. But I look back at that time and cringe. My general routine: wake up around nine; roll into the office around ten; work until seven with maybe/probably a stop for happy hour; grab a sandwich (and usually cigarettes) at 7-Eleven on the way home; go out to a concert or two; come home after the bars closed at two; write until three or four; sleep; repeat. I slept on the couch, because it was too hot in my bedroom from the broken shower, and generally did not take care of myself at all. I'd stay up for two days at a time and I knew the clerks on every shift at probably three separate 7-Elevens. My favorite guy, who worked late nights and with whom I had developed a bit of a friendship, disappeared suddenly. I didn't see him again for two years, until I was working as a cater waiter at a corporate Christmas party, doing a one-off favor for a friend. They sent me out into a driving rainstorm to buy fifty dollar's worth of ice at a nearby liquor store. When I walked in, there he was. I don't mind telling you that when I wiped the rain out of my eyes and saw him, we hugged. Dallas is sometimes, a lot of times, the biggest small town you'll ever find.

One night, and I promise I'm not proud of this, I came home,

sat down on the couch after being awake for thirty-six hours, and called my then-girlfriend. I told her to come over in an hour, I just needed to shower and change clothes. And as soon as I hung up, I passed out, more unconscious than asleep. My body had mutinied.

An hour later, my girlfriend came over and couldn't get me to answer, so she called, and I didn't pick up the phone, either, even though the phone was maybe three inches from my face. She kept trying, banging on the door, calling me, and after an hour called my best friend, Josh, to help. He was at work, so he recruited another guy we knew, who came over. And for two hours, Josh called every two minutes while they kicked the door; imagine sleeping through paint being mixed above your head. Finally, I woke up and very casually answered the phone, unaware of what had been transpiring outside of my apartment. Josh angrily told me to open the door, and so I did, and my girlfriend called me an asshole and left.

The next day, I came home and sat down on the couch—and passed out again, sleeping through the semisecret Cheap Trick show at Trees that I had planned on attending.

I'd like to say that incident was wildly uncharacteristic of that time in my life, but the truth is that it wasn't too out of the ordinary. I have a lot of stories like that. I could have used some basketball in my life. I could have used a couple of hours every night or two just *watching* people be active. That would have been a start.

⊕   ⊕   ⊕

Remember what you said when the lockout ended? "Shit, it's actually going to happen."

You had gone back to Würzburg to play for the X-Rays and you were living with your parents. Nothing had changed after the Mavericks drafted you; it was almost like it hadn't happened. Since you made the choice to come over and play in Dallas back in June, you hadn't thought about it and you hadn't had to. When the lockout ended, you finally had to confront your feelings, and you were a little scared.

It was, as you might put it, *a big step, obviously*. You were playing for a team whose gym seated 3,500. The X-Rays had been promoted to play in the Basketball Bundesliga first division, but it was still small-time. On opening night, you played Alba Berlin, whose coach, Svetislav Pešić, was talking shit about you going to the NBA. His players said they'd hold you to single digits. You still got an easy seventeen; no one could check you, even as a skinny twenty-year-old. By the time the lockout ended and it was time to come to Dallas, you were leading the Bundesliga in scoring[2] and thinking about moving to a bigger club, a tougher league, if you had to stay in Europe any longer. (You also played your first three games for the German senior team, leading them in scoring twice even though you came off the bench all three games.)

You had made one quick trip to Dallas, in December, so you

---

2. Averaging more than twenty-one points a game, along with 8.3 rebounds, which was second in the league.

could find a place to live and start getting to know your teammates on and off the court. You worked out with Nash and Chris Anstey, the team's first-round pick the year before you, and you played in pickup games with some of the other guys and former Mavericks like Derek Harper. Holger told the *Morning News* that you now felt like you had "a chance to make it in the NBA." Harper had a simpler assessment: "He can shoot the hell out of the ball."

X-Rays fans got their last chance to see you do that on January 9, 1999. You were sick—if it wasn't the flu, it was close enough—but you played anyway. You could have saved yourself for the NBA, but you didn't hold anything back. Have you ever? Würzburg was down seven points with 3:20 left, and then you hit three three-pointers and a free throw for a one-point win.

Two days later, you got a new visa and caught the next flight to Dallas.

And the Mavs didn't make it easy on you when you arrived, did they? Nellie said, "I had Chris Mullin"—the Hall of Fame forward and member of the Dream Team who played for him at Golden State—"and I love him to death, but he doesn't have this guy's skills." He softened that, somewhat, adding, "I preface everything by saying if he can't do it at twenty, he'll do it at twenty-one. Or twenty-two. All he needs is maturity and experience. I'll give him the opportunity to get those two things."

It was time to walk into the typhoon.

⊕　⊕　⊕

It didn't really matter what the Nelsons said about you, because almost two decades of history, very little of it positive, preceded your arrival. I'm not sure you really knew what you had to overcome, and it was better that way, I know. Before we go on, I just want to take a moment to underline it, if you don't mind.

A SHORT HISTORY OF (MOSTLY) TALL WHITE STIFFS IN DALLAS MAVERICKS HISTORY, 1980–1998

<u>Kurt Nimphius</u>: As unlikely as it would seem, even though there were only twenty-four teams in the NBA after the Mavericks joined the league in 1980, and far fewer jobs to go around, there was still more than enough room for guys like Nimphius, whose most useful skill was that he was six foot ten. His brightest highlights for the Mavs were: not getting completely washed when he got into a fistfight with Hakeem Olajuwon during Hakeem's rookie season, and then later getting traded for James Donaldson, who was better at everything, including wearing the No. 40 jersey. Nimphius was, at his absolute very best, competent. When I come across a photo of him, he looks like either former Mavs guard Brad Davis was injected with Super-Soldier Serum (if it's from his days in Dallas, 1981 to 1985, when he had short hair and an insurance adjuster's mustache), or a member of REO Speedwagon playing pickup ball in jeans while on tour (if it's after the trade and he grew his hair big rather than long, a lion's mane that appeared carved rather than cut).

<u>Bill Garnett</u>: The first player taken in the 1982 draft was James Worthy, a Hall of Famer. The second was Terry Cummings, who

would be named Rookie of the Year and make two All-NBA teams in his very solid eighteen seasons. The third was Dominique Wilkins, another Hall of Famer with an all-time great nickname (the Human Highlight Reel). The fourth, chosen by the upstart Mavs, was Garnett, a power forward and center out of the University of Wyoming who lasted only four years in the NBA and just two in Dallas. In fairness to the Mavs, there were only three stars in that draft. On the other hand, Sleepy Floyd, Fat Lever, Trent Tucker, Rick Pierce, Paul Pressey, Scott Hastings, Rod Higgins, Fred Roberts, Craig Hodges, Terry Teagle, Cliff Levingston, and Mark Eaton—all selected after Garnett—went on to have productive careers. (On the *other* other hand, Garnett was at least better than the Mavs' other picks that year: Corny Thompson, Rudy Woods, Ken Arnold, Wayne Waggoner, Bob Grady, Keith Peterson, Ralph McPherson, and Albert Culton. They did ten-round (!) drafts back then. Those guys combined to play a total of forty-four games in the NBA.)

<u>Uwe Blab and Bill Wennington:</u> Somehow in the 1985 draft, the first to feature a lottery drawing to award the top pick, the Mavs took two of the first three German players in NBA history.[3] The first, of course you know: Detlef Schrempf, chosen at No. 8. We'll talk more about him soon, but he turned out to be a very good player, just not with

3. The third was Christian Welp, drafted by the Philadelphia 76ers in 1987. He lasted only three seasons (with Philly, San Antonio, and Golden State) but had a very successful career in Europe.

the Mavericks. The coaching staff didn't know what to do with him, and his only real sin was that he wasn't Karl Malone. The future Hall of Fame forward from Louisiana really wanted to play in Dallas and he made sure to take it out on the team whenever he played against them, reminding them that they passed on him to take Schrempf. After Schrempf, the Mavs chose centers Blab (from Germany) and Wennington (from Canada) back-to-back at Nos. 17 and 18. Blab was the first and the worst of the two selections, ending his five-year stint in the league with averages of 2.1 points and 1.8 rebounds. Wennington managed a fifteen-year career, most notably as a towel-waving backup center on the Chicago Bulls' bench during three championship seasons. And he is in the Canadian Basketball Hall of Fame, but that was a pretty empty building for a long time, no offense to anyone. In 1988, his best season with the Mavs, Wennington averaged 4.6 points and 4.4 rebounds.

Jim Farmer and Steve Alford: In 1987, the Mavs picked Farmer a couple of spots ahead of the late Reggie Lewis, who died at the Celtics' practice gym in 1993, so they at least avoided that heartbreak. With everything that was going on with Roy Tarpley, that might have been too much for the franchise to bear. It was almost too much, anyway. But you don't love to see a first-round choice have more success as a country singer, especially when he didn't have that much success as a country singer. Alford, a lights-out shooter who had a standout college career at Indiana under Noted Dickhead™ Bobby Knight, wasn't big enough or fast enough or good enough to stick in the NBA

and looked more like a model for plastic combs. He got into coaching pretty quickly.

Cherokee Parks and Loren Meyer: Both joined the Mavs in 1995. Parks's sister, also very tall, used to play bass in a band called Nashville Pussy. The Duke product only lasted one disappointing season with the Mavs before being traded, so I don't have a lot to work with. Meyer scored 645 points in his NBA career. Why do these things come in twos?

Shawn Bradley: I don't think there has ever been a player in the history of the NBA, or maybe in the history of professional basketball, that players have enjoyed dunking on more than the seven foot six Bradley, who was built like one of those floppy inflatable tube men they put in front of car dealerships, and wasn't quite as aggressive. Shaquille O'Neal probably still dreams of doing it. I was at the American Airlines Center on the night in the 2005 playoffs when Tracy McGrady all but ended his career, jumping on him like a little kid getting a piggyback ride to a swing set. It was like witnessing a murder.

(There are a lot of other names I could mention here: Bruno Šundov, seven foot three, drafted the same year as you, fairly generic then, now looks like someone Keanu Reeves would acrobatically kill in a movie; Greg Dreiling, who came through twice and who I still get confused with my son's old pediatrician; Eric Montross, who averaged just slightly more points than personal fouls in forty-

seven games; Martin Müürsepp, who was part of the trade that brought Nash to Dallas, accounted for almost all of the umlauts in team history and is the only Estonian to ever play in the NBA. The Mavericks—and Nellie in particular—kept gambling that one of these Clark Kents was actually Superman. There were others before and there would be more after. But let's skip straight to the one who made it the hardest for you.)

Chris Anstey: He was another alleged savior from foreign shores who was supposed to deliver us from misery and instead just moved a rollaway bed into it. I know you were friends, but it's true. The Australian was drafted the year before you and was essentially promised to be you: a mobile (Nellie called him "the best running big man in the NBA"), knockdown-shooting seven-footer. At least Nellie knew what he was looking for. Both you and Anstey were tennis players before switching sports—he did it much later, not seriously picking up a basketball until he was seventeen—and he even vaguely resembled you, especially when you first came over. So a casual fan, which is just about all the Mavs had then, could have been forgiven if he couldn't tell if the team had really drafted two different players. Anstey only survived two seasons in Dallas and one more in Chicago and then left the NBA, going first to Russia and then back to Australia, where he enjoyed a fine career, winning two Australian NBL MVP awards and finally retiring in 2010.

It is unfair that, because of timing and proximity, he has to be judged against one of the best ever. Most things are unfair.

2

And Sometime Soon Be Better Than You Were

It was perhaps a little too perfect that your first real NBA game, on February 5, 1999, was against the Seattle Supersonics—the home, at the time, of the previous most famous German basketball player, Detlef Schrempf. Wouldn't you agree? Your story is littered with these little narrative flourishes that might cause an editor to narrow her eyes, worry that it's getting a little too cute. Your entire first season, really, is an armory of Chekhov's guns, all waiting to go off at some point over the next twenty years, as well as other names and places that will cohere into themes, and some that will reappear later as callbacks and Easter eggs, rewarding the careful reader.

(Your first game in Dallas, a preseason contest on January 30, featured the same opponent as your final one, on April 9, 2019: the Phoenix Suns. For example. It's like a sports movie where they only show three teams to keep down costs.)

But so anyway: Detlef. He'd told a German TV station that he knew nothing about you except that you were "from a little village" and cautioned you to "stay away from women and drugs." You hadn't met yet, and he claimed he hadn't even seen you play, and

your countrymen took the thirty-six-year-old Schrempf's seem-
ing aloofness to mean you were already rivals. Why hadn't he taken
you under his wing, or at least offered you encouragement? But you
waved it away. "Nah, I don't think so," you said when people asked
if there was tension. You told Marc Stein that everyone in Germany
loved Schrempf but the "kids have other role models," and everyone
knew that your guy was Scottie Pippen. I only wish this had happened in the social media era, with people reacting to Schrempf's
shade by tweeting the Mariah Carey "I don't know her" GIF but
with "Ich kenne sie nicht" written over it.

To you, the whole deal was mostly just a hassle: "I wanted to
play someone else first—some Americans." Wasn't it enough for
everyone, for the universe, for the basketball gods, that it was your
first game?

You weren't nervous beforehand, not until you gathered with
the other starters at center court for the opening tip and started slapping hands and you realized where you were and what was about
to happen. And you didn't even realize what was actually about to
happen, just the abstract. If you'd known you were going to score
just two points—to go with zero rebounds—in sixteen minutes, you
might have rushed past nervousness and straight into terror. It was
fine up until the game began. You met Detlef at the morning shoot-
araound at KeyArena and he said he'd give you his phone number in
case you needed help adjusting. He meant off the court, but maybe
you considered giving him a call at halftime after you hadn't made
a single shot. You didn't in the second half either, just a pair of free

throws early in the third. You sat the entirety of the fourth quarter and overtime, watching the rest of a six-point loss.

Your parents were watching back in Würzburg—they had rushed around to find the correct cable converter—along with your girlfriend, Sybille Gerer (a forward on the same club team your sister Silke played on), and some other relatives. Tip-off was 4:00 a.m. Saturday morning in Germany. Maybe you wished they had slept in. You didn't say much after; there wasn't much to talk about. But you were honest as ever, saying that for someone as tall as you "to get no rebounds in sixteen minutes is unbelievable."

"He's tall, he's white, and he's German, so of course he's going to be called the next Detlef Schrempf," said the current Detlef Schrempf. (Again, I wish this had happened during the social media era. I absolutely would have tweeted two Spider-Men pointing at each other but both crudely repainted like the German flag.) "But he's going to be his own player."

Back at the hotel, Donnie Nelson went over the game with you, practically frame by frame. You did it right, remembering everything you needed to remember and forgetting everything you needed to forget. Two nights later, against Golden State, Nellie put you on Muggsy Bogues, the Warriors' five-foot-three point guard, and you couldn't help but get five easy first-quarter rebounds, on your way to twelve for the game. And you made your first two shots. You'd finish with sixteen points, and it was a little rough at the end, with some late turnovers, but your Mavs won, 102–99 in double overtime. And you'd played well! Maybe it was because you were

familiar with the gym. You'd been there during your recruiting trip to Cal, watching one of their games at the future Oracle Arena as well as a Warriors practice.

Before the home opener at Reunion Arena, you asked fans to be patient with you, and perhaps you were asking that of yourself, too. The schedule did you no favors. The pace was insane. Fifteen games in the first twenty-three days. Nine of the first eleven on the road. A run of nine games in thirteen days, from February 11–23. No one did you any favors, really. Nellie was touting you as a Rookie of the Year contender and his son was saying you would "revolutionize the game." Meanwhile, Paul Pierce, taken one pick after you, was up in Boston looking like a real ROY candidate.

You were having your moments: fifteen and nine in that home debut against future Hall of Famers Karl Malone and John Stockton and the Utah Jazz, coming off two straight Finals appearances; eight in the first quarter against Houston, including an and-one against your idol, Scottie Pippen, in his first season with the Rockets. But they were moments, not stretches. Those were difficult to put together because you were tired and disoriented. "I've never been a week on the road without seeing home," you said, nine days into an eleven-day road trip.

You were averaging 8.8 points and 4.8 rebounds, shooting just under 35 percent, and some columnists and beat writers were (cautiously) bringing up Portland taking Sam Bowie over Michael Jordan in 1984 while Pierce got off to a fast start with the Celtics. On February 20, you were taken out of the starting lineup in favor

of veteran Cedric Ceballos. "Nowitzki sitski," one knucklehead columnist[4] wrote. Did you see that one? A couple of games later, including one in which you missed seven of eight shots in ten minutes, you didn't play at all. You didn't like coming off the bench, finding it too hard to get into a groove, and you didn't particularly like the United States right then, unsurprisingly. "I don't think when I'm old I'll be here," you told the *Star-Telegram*. "And when the season ends, I'm gone."

But, nonetheless, you were—slowly—finding your way, sort of. You were living in the same townhouse complex as teammates Hubert Davis, Chris Anstey, and Nash, over where the sprawling West Village shopping center is now. Before it had been developed, it was a big park; Davis walked his dog there. It was something like home. Anstey was your friend, and Nash was more like a brother. He taught you how to write checks, a task you were unfamiliar with, having never done it before. He lived four houses down, and you had his garage code, so you could pop in, see what was going on. And there was always something.

"I think for some reason he has ADD bad," you told me in 2009. "He can't just sit in the hotel room at night. There has to be some action going on. Which was great for me, because I didn't want to sit in the hotel room every road trip, or at home all the time."

There was an Albertson's supermarket a block or so away and you'd make midnight runs to the deserted store for Sprite and

---

4. Richie Whitt. He doesn't deserve more than a footnote.

something to satisfy your sweet tooth; you hadn't figured out a healthy diet yet. You didn't go out to bars much—that would come—because you'd get carded and also because American beer tasted "like lemonade" to you, as you told the *Star-T* in March. By then, you were the ninth man in the Mavs' rotation. But it was OK, because around that time your dad came over, with Silke's boyfriend. It was Jörg-Werner Nowitzki's first time in America. You bought him a bed and sheets and pillows from Target.

Remember what he said when he was interviewed at halftime of his first Mavericks game? "Hello, Dallas Mavericks! I love you!"

At the end of March, you played in San Antonio—almost exactly a year after your Hoop Summit appearance there. It's all a little too perfect, like I said. Your story is unbelievable, and I mean that in every sense. In the movie version, San Antonio is where everything would click. You'd rediscover your Hoop Summit form and everything would go from there. But it wasn't always so neat and tidy. At twenty years old, you weren't quite ready yet. You scored just two points in twelve minutes of a twenty-two-point loss. But you were philosophical about it: "I'm so young. When I'll be twenty-two or twenty-three, I think I'll be alright."

And Detlef agreed. You faced him again during the last game in March and you put up respectable numbers that time.[5] "He's gone as far as he was going to go in Germany," Schrempf said. "I think if he wanted to prove himself, he made the right decision. As far as what

---

5. You had eleven points and seven rebounds in seventeen minutes.

everybody says, he's got a lot of talent and he works hard. So it's just a matter of time before he establishes himself and gets more playing time."

But still, it had to be difficult for you, Pierce up in Boston getting eighteen, nineteen a game and in Dallas they're saying things like DNP–Dirk No Play. People booed you at Reunion Arena, while other fans wanted your autograph or to take a picture with you, and you didn't understand either reaction. Nothing made sense!

And then:

Nellie surprisingly put you back in the starting lineup for another game against the Spurs on April 13. (In the movie, let's just combine them.) The Mavs won 92–86 and you hit a fadeaway in the lane over Tim Duncan to give the team an 84-81 lead with 2:28 left and then the clinching free throw with 15 seconds left. You only scored twelve points, but it was a different twelve points, a *significant* twelve points.

AND

THEN

Your first great game.

April 16, thirty-six games into your rookie season. The Mavericks lost to the Suns, but you went for twenty-nine points, fifteen in the second half, and eight rebounds. "I've been waiting for this for a long time," you said. "It was tough this whole year. The first couple of games were alright, but then I fell into a deep hole, and I didn't come out of it for a long time."

Holger had come back to Dallas, after two months away and a bout of measles. And just in time: you were down, your shot was off, nothing was right. But then Holger was there again, showing you the tools, and you were out of that deep hole. Your twenty-two points (on ten of thirteen shooting) and three assists fueled a huge road win against the Rockets. ("Scottie Pippen is my favorite player of all time. To play against him was really fun," you said, pointing out that Pippen did not defend you.) You finished off a deciding 10–2 run against Vancouver with two baskets. Another twenty-two against Houston and another win. An efficient fifteen against Golden State.

The season would end exactly where it began, literally and maybe spiritually, in Seattle against the Sonics. You were a little better, with nine points and five rebounds, but you also shot just two for thirteen from the floor and had six turnovers. (The other disappointing end to the season: your truly awful rookie card. You had been so excited to see it, but it looked like they'd pasted your head on Anstey's body.) But it was over. You'd made it. Maybe just barely. There had been times when you'd talked to forward Gary Trent on the plane about going home, perhaps even before the season was over. But you held fast.

And you'd improved, finishing strong.[6] You didn't just escape.

---

6. After your last DNP on April 1, you'd averaged almost twelve points and fiverebounds on 45 percent shooting over seventeen games. If we only count the last fourteen, when you were a starter again, it's even better: 13.6 points, 5.2 rebounds. Over the last twelve, it was 14.5 points, 4.8 rebounds, and 47.4 percent shooting.

You had learned what you had to. One, that the game here was more physical; everyone was more aggressive.

Two, that you could play it.

⊕ ⊕ ⊕

You came back to Dallas for a minicamp to get ready for summer league in Los Angeles and Salt Lake City, during which the team planned to make you its main ball handler. While there, you reflected on your first season with Stein.

"This year was pretty frustrating, the hardest thing in basketball I went through, for sure. At least I had a couple good games at the end that showed I could compete at this level."

And once you knew that, you were ready.

Even before your second season began, you were ready. You went with the other young guys to play summer league ball, and everyone knew you were the best there, and not just on the Mavs' squad. The best, period. As your teammate Greg Buckner put it, you "put on a fucking show." You turned L.A. and Salt Lake City into Bavarian villages, dominating like you were back in the Bundesliga. Everything the Nelsons talked about, and everything you hinted at as your rookie season wound down, it was all there.

It made sense that it took some time to adjust. You'd never heard of illegal defense. You didn't know what a shootaround was until you asked Gary Trent. He told you it was like a rehearsal. Then you had to ask him what a rehearsal was. You didn't have time to prepare,

had to learn everything in a week, the terminology, the nuances, the speed—all while living on your own for the first time. It was like you were playing every game while trying to comfort an infant you were carrying around in a BabyBjörn, and then you had to sit down and take a calculus test immediately after.

It didn't help that your shot didn't arrive right away, like it had been in your luggage and ended up in another plane's cargo hold, and you were making do with a gift-shop version. But Holger came back at the end of October and got you straightened out. You explained then what his presence meant to you, and that's the way it would be going forward: "He helps me get my rhythm back and he tells me what I have to do."

After just nine points in the first game of your second season, against Golden State, you had fifteen against Seattle, and twenty each against Golden State (again) and the Lakers, and you were rolling. "I think it's getting better for me from game to game," you said after the return engagement with the Warriors. "I finally learned how to play harder and to stay aggressive. I just wasn't used to hitting the boards and diving for balls. I didn't have to that in Germany."

Maybe it would have all gone differently if Trent hadn't torn his hamstring. But he did, and you replaced him in the starting lineup at power forward and made the most of it.[7] As you started to come into your own, guys tested you. Steve Francis tossed you to the court in a

---

7. Averaging sixteen points and 6.3 rebounds on 54.8 percent shooting, including 67 percent from three.

November game against the Rockets. "I've never been in a fight in my life," you admitted, but people probably already knew. You got your payback on the court. Exactly a week later, you gave Francis and the Rockets a career-high thirty-one points.

You tied that mark a few weeks later, got thirty against the Lakers after Christmas, and set a new high (thirty-two) in April against the Nuggets. And just as you got better as the 1999–2000 season went on, so did the Mavericks. The team ended with a 40–42 record, losing but still its best mark in years, and closed on a 16–5 surge. "It's sad that this team did not make the playoffs, but we've shown that we're capable of playing that well," you said when it was over. You wouldn't have to talk about missing the playoffs again until 2013.

At least part of the positive energy had something to do with Mark Cuban buying the team halfway through the season, paying $285 million for a majority stake on January 4, 2000. I knew Cuban as the guy whose expensive car might be parked in front of the Broadcast.com building in Deep Ellum when I went there to record a weekly internet radio show I cohosted that I doubt anyone ever listened to. (It was called *Scene Heard Radio*, after the weekly column I wrote for the *Observer*, and we talked about music and played songs. It was essentially a podcast before podcasts.) I remember right after Cuban sold Broadcast to Yahoo!, making him a billionaire and most of the employees rich; at least for a while; the woman who produced our show was distracted because she was pricing Jaguars. Cuban had more impact on you and the Mavs in the years to come, but his presence immediately made the franchise

feel exciting for the first time in a decade. The Mavericks were interesting again.

Can you believe that he brought Dennis Rodman home to Dallas for twelve chaotic games? He even tried to skirt the salary cap by having the mercurial Rodman—a tireless rebounder and champion with Detroit and Chicago with hair like a mood ring, which somehow was the most normal thing about him—live at his house. OK, so maybe you guys finished strong in spite of Cuban buying the team. But no one could say he wasn't willing to try whatever it might take.

But most of the reason why the Mavs got better was simple: you. You basically doubled your averages in every category[8] while starting eighty-one of eighty-two games. It was all enough to earn a second-place finish in the Most Improved Player voting behind Indiana Pacers guard Jalen Rose.

And with that, the preamble was over.

---

8. From 8.2 points to 17.5; from 3.4 rebounds to 6.5; from 1 assist per game to 2.5. Your shooting percentages increased from 40.5 to 46, and from behind the arc it went from 21 percent to 38.

3

I Want a Name That Can Cut Glass

When you were drafted, you were *Dirk? Nowitzki?* and you kept the question marks throughout your rookie season, their meaning changing at some point from *unknown* to *unlikely*. Your second year, you'd leveled up to simply Dirk Nowitzki, earning the cautious trust of a fanbase that had experienced Jennifer-Aniston-on-the-cover-of-*US-Weekly*-and-is-she-ever-going-to-find-happiness-and-a-*baby*? levels of heartbreak for a decade.

And then, in your third season, you became **DIRK**.

You started all eighty-two games and led the team in scoring, rebounds, and three-pointers made, averaging 21.8 points, 9.2 rebounds, 2.1 assists, 1.2 blocks, and 1 steal, with 151 three-pointers on 39 percent shooting. No seven-footer had ever done all of that at once, and none have since.[9] You were named to the All-NBA third team, the first Maverick to achieve that honor, yet somehow didn't

---

9. Nine times a player has hit those averages with more than a hundred threes. You did it six of those times. Karl-Anthony Towns has done it twice, and Nikola Jokić once. (You also fell just short twice more, with ninety-nine and ninety-one threes.)

make the All-Star roster. (You being you, you wouldn't even consider it a snub.) And you, along with Michael Finley and Steve Nash, led the Mavs back to the playoffs, winning fifty-three games and finishing fifth in the Western Conference.

Your second year, you proved you belonged in the league. Your third year, you proved you'd be a star. You *were* a star. It was all happening.

⊕ ⊕ ⊕

By then, you'd become Americanized, at least a little bit, as you got more comfortable, peppering your speech with phrases like "Holler at a player, yo." Nash said you were "definitely a cross between MTV and BET." Maybe you cringe a little bit hearing that now, but it's funny. People were starting to see your personality, the other guys, how you'd bust on them in the locker room.

The Mavs were still mostly Finley's team then, and he'd earned that. The six-foot-seven guard came to Dallas in the 1996–97 season, and when the team finally made it back to the playoffs, he was twenty-seven, right in his prime, perfectly positioned to be Dallas's Michael Jordan. He was the right size, grew up in the suburbs of Chicago, and had been handpicked by Jordan himself to be one of the original five members of Team Jordan when it became its own brand under the Nike umbrella in 1997. Finley was an All-Star in 2000 and 2001 and the guy who wanted the ball at the end of games. He was a twenty-point-a-game scorer, an alpha dog straight out of the *NBA on NBC*

1990s, just missing "Roundball Rock" intros and softball Ahmad Rashad interviews.

But the league was changing, as it always has and always will. There weren't any players like Jordan when he came around in 1984, and then there were too many, none as good, all created in His image. Every singer-songwriter was the New Dylan and every six-foot-six wing who could jump at all was Baby Jordan. It was time for a new model to emulate, and that new model, for a while, would be you.

Nominally, in 2000–01, you were still part of Dallas's "Big Three," with Finley and Nash. And that worked for you, being able to slink into the background, let Mike and Steve get some of the attention—or most of it, if you were lucky. If Finley was the team's Jordan, perfect. You wanted to be its Scottie Pippen, anyway. Even better, Cuban was getting more attention than the three of you combined.

It would change. It was changing. In fact, it had changed. The transition was a tectonic shift, below the surface and almost imperceptible, but just as certain. The Mavs weren't officially your team until 2004–05, but everyone in Dallas knew it was yours in May 2001. It had been coming all season. You were starting to put up serious numbers, and consistently.[10] The team's success and the exciting style of play that brought it about, the running and gunning and threes and dunking, made the Mavs popular as a whole, and that obscured what was happening. Maybe no one was ready to fully buy

---

10. You had thirty-one in Boston and New Jersey, thirty-five in Houston, and thirty-six (another new career high) in Philly.

into a twenty-two-year-old kid from Germany yet. There wasn't any precedent. So all bets were hedged. When you made a cameo in the Lil Bow Wow vehicle *Like Mike* (released in the summer of 2002), it was alongside Finley and Nash.[11] And when *Sports Illustrated* ran its first big "let's meet the Mavs" feature, you were photographed with Finley, Nash, Cuban, and big man Juwan Howard.

This is where the iconic cowboy hat photos came from. When I think about your early years, I think about this photo shoot. Out of the handful that have been made public, two stand out. One is a group shot, Finley and Howard holding black cowboy hats, you and Nash wearing them, and you riding on Cuban's back. The other is just you and Cuban, both in hats. He's got a lasso around your torso and you're looking away, smiling. Do I have a shirt with one of these on it? Maybe I do.

(Also! For that same story, as I'm sure you recall, there is a photo of Cuban posing in front of Finley's locker, wearing only one of the plush new personalized towels that he'd bought for the team. I wonder how hard it was for photographer Jeffrey Lowe to convince Cuban to pose for that shot. I'm guessing not very, and, honestly, if I owned a sports franchise, was single and in shape, as Cuban was then, I would do it, too.)

The *Sports Illustrated* photos were goofy and a little sweet and they showed that you were up for anything, and that would never

---

11. Though for some reason, on the poster it was just you and Nash, alongside Allen Iverson, Jason Kidd, Chris Webber, and Morris Chestnut.

really change. It was a good way for the world at large to get introduced to the new version of the Mavs after the team had spent the previous decade in the basketball Bermuda Triangle.

But the photo I think about the most when I think about your early years did not come from that shoot, though it was part of the reason why *SI* commissioned it. This photo was taken a few months earlier. In it, you are on the court at Reunion Arena, Game 4 of the Western Conference semifinals against the San Antonio Spurs, the first time the Mavs had been in the second round since 1988. You have a faraway look on your face, blindly slapping hands with someone out of frame, your mouth bloody—not gruesomely but noticeably. You were still playing even though you'd gotten your two front teeth knocked out, after taking an elbow from Spurs guard Terry Porter in the fourth quarter.

This is when you became **DIRK** to me. There was no denying that you were a man, no denying that you were The Man. Dallas, as a city, has often been dismissed as superficial, full of glitz but not grit, and that criticism has been extended to its basketball team and especially you as its leader. But after that game against the Spurs, we no longer had any questions about what you were made of. You were tough, and that made us tough. We wanted to see ourselves in you, and wanted the world to see us in you, too.

I remember seeing this photo of you the next morning in the paper, and in that moment all doubt was removed for me. The season would end one game later, but I knew there would be more. There would be better, because you were here, and you were just getting

started. I was back, all in, a full-time Mavs fan again. Ready to be hurt—and I would be—but it was OK.

⊕   ⊕   ⊕

My full-fledged return to the Mavericks had been coming. Ten days earlier, I was at the Gypsy Tea Room in Deep Ellum, working, waiting to see a musician from Austin named David Garza. (You'd probably like him; start with *This Euphoria* from 1998.) Garza had to postpone his set because everyone was crowded around the bar, watching the TV hanging above it, as Game 5 against the Utah Jazz, the deciding game of the first-round series, came to a close. You didn't have a great shooting night, but you'd kept the team in it from the free-throw line, taking and making ten as the Mavs came back from being behind by seventeen, after having been down 2–0 in the series. I remember when Calvin Booth made his only shot, after Finley passed out of a double team and found him near the basket for the game-winner, and the shotgun blast of sound from the crowd around the bar, the way it made everything move in slow motion and fast forward at the same time, like jumping off a cliff into deep water, adrenaline coursing through your veins, every sense at its absolute peak. You're operating at 100 percent capacity but only for a moment.

I didn't think that was how the series would end. After the first game, it seemed like the veteran Jazz team was too experienced, and maybe you weren't quite ready for the playoffs. The Mavs had a lead going into the fourth quarter, but you missed three of four shots and

a free throw and had four turnovers. You still had a chance to win it at the end, but even though you were open for a straight-on three, you passed to a double-teamed Finley without even considering it. "Maybe I should've looked at the hoop," you said, "but you're always smarter afterward, aren't you?" On one crucial play, Karl Malone stripped you cleanly with that swiping move you would add to your arsenal later. Game 2 was worse. You only made three shots and the crowd booed you every time you touched the ball because you'd said Salt Lake City was "a bad city." (Which, fair.) So that was new. You'd never faced an angry crowd like that. And there was so much pressure, anyway, since Dallas hadn't won a playoff game in thirteen years.

Before Game 3, you went to the gym three nights in a row.

You were brand new again.

You had twenty-four points by halftime, thirty-three for the game. *Let's roll, baby*, you said to yourself after one jumper, psyching yourself up. That was just a warmup for Game 4. You had thirty-three again, but effortlessly this time, making ten of nineteen shots, including five threes, in a thirty-point win that set up Game 5 and Booth's winning basket.

Your first of many playoff games against the Spurs was next, and it was forgettable, just nine points while struggling with foul trouble. Of your teammates, only Howard Eisley, of all people, played well. The next two games weren't much better. After a bout with food poisoning, you needed to be hooked up to an IV (twice) to even make it out on the court for Game 3. If you'd given up then, it would have been OK. The season was already a success. Fifty-three wins.

A victory in a playoff series. But you could never leave it like that, could you?

Game 4 was yours. Thirty points on eleven of eighteen shooting and perfect eight of eight from the line, with nine rebounds, one assist, and two missing teeth, thanks to Porter's elbow. Juwan Howard said you looked like a hockey player; you only missed thirty-three seconds of game time.

"What a gutsy guy," Nellie said.

And what did you say?

"If people want to call me soft, they can call me soft. I'm not doing this to shut people up. I came back out there because we had to win this game. We had too good a season to get swept."

You went out on your shield, scoring a career-high forty-two points (twenty-eight more than any other teammate) and grabbing eighteen rebounds, playing all but one minute and demanding the ball in the second half. Even with only 2:25 left and the Mavs down eighteen, you were clapping and yelling, "Let's go!" like a miracle might happen. You played until you couldn't play anymore.

Until they wouldn't let you.

⊕   ⊕   ⊕

Before the 2001–02 season, Nellie said, "I think Dirk knows he's good. I don't think he knows how good."

The Mavs knew. They signed you to a six-year contract worth around $90 million on October 23. And then you somehow got

better again, averaging more points (23.4) and rebounds (9.9) while upping all your shooting percentages. In May, you became the first Maverick to appear on the cover of *Sports Illustrated*, under the headline "Style Points." (You had never heard of the *SI* cover jinx.) You played in your first All-Star game and made the All-NBA second team. You finished eighth in MVP voting. The team got better, too, winning fifty-seven games and sweeping Kevin Garnett and the Minnesota Timberwolves in the first round of the playoffs. Yet you still hadn't made the team yours.

"You never know who's going to take the crunch-time shot," you said, after the first game against Minnesota, when you had thirty and fifteen. "That's the beauty about being on this team right now." But how could you deny it would be you, or *should* be you? How could anyone? By the end of the series, you'd had four straight games of at least thirty points and fifteen rebounds, the first to do that since Kareem Abdul-Jabbar in 1977. We were all ready for you to take over. Why didn't you?

The team needed you to take over. The season would end in five games in the second round, again, this time at the hands of the Sacramento Kings. The Kings, at that time, were the Mavericks' spiritual twin, an offensive juggernaut that played the game beautifully, aesthetically perfect on one end, employing a whirring version of the Princeton offense, a system predicated on passing and cutting and guile, a different roadmap to the same destination as the Mavs[12]—only

---

12. You were part of the No. 1 offense that season.

they were, at that time, more successful. They had the best record in
the league and would have gone to the Finals that season if not for a
wildly controversial, and some have suggested actually criminal, finish to the Western Conference finals against the Lakers. The Kings
had two of the best passing big men in NBA history, in Chris Webber
and Vlade Divac; a solid point guard in Mike Bibby; the terrifying Peja
Stojaković, who always seemed to get open just long enough to shove
a knife between the Mavs' ribs; and the supremely irritating Doug
Christie, who was as good on defense as he was at making complicated
hand gestures to his wife in the stands, which is to say: *extremely*.

The series was tied after two games, and it looked like it would
live up to its potential as a shootout between two great offensive
teams and two franchises on their way up.

But you couldn't get into a rhythm, thanks to the Kings making
you their No. 1 priority on defense, harassing you everywhere, dou-
ble-teaming you. You weren't prepared for that, weren't aggressive
enough, couldn't pass your way out of it. After Game 3, Nellie said,
"I don't like to see Dirk with this kind of a physical and mental down
period right now." He met with you half an hour the next day, trying to
get you through it. It worked, but it was too late. You had thirty-one,
twelve, and seven in an overtime loss in Game 4, which you almost sent
into a second overtime, and you were even better in Game 5, finishing
with thirty-two. You almost won that one on your own, scoring eight
straight points in the third to cut the lead to one. But you didn't get a
shot or even touch the ball as the Kings answered with seven consecutive points of their own, and that was it. The Mavs lost by thirteen, and

the season was done. You left without talking to reporters. Two weeks later, you had surgery to remove bone spurs from your left ankle, a lingering injury you had been playing through all season.

Would it have made a difference if you had been 100 percent healthy? Probably not, and I doubt you'd use that excuse. All you knew was that the same result a year later wasn't good enough this time.

⊕   ⊕   ⊕

It wasn't uncommon to see you, almost always with Steve, here and there in those first few years, when you were both young and wild and free. When we all were.

"It was a different time," you told me once. "The Mavericks, in the nineties, had a tough decade. We'd go somewhere all the time and people were like, 'Oh, you're tall,' but they had no idea who I was. And Steve, obviously, being so small, he could just blend in."

Maybe too well. My friend Gavin remembers repeatedly kicking Steve in the leg—"hard," he says—one night at The Loon, a bar down the street from your townhouse. He thought it was a bar stool.

I had gotten married at the end of 2000—somewhat on a whim; we told each other we could always get divorced; we eventually did—but I was out just as much, doing the same dumb things, but never at the same place or at least not at the same time. Given how small Dallas can be, it's honestly a little surprising. You and Steve weren't there the night in May 2000 when I playfully put Robbie Van Winkle (better known as

Vanilla Ice) into a headlock after an Elliott Smith show at Trees in Deep Ellum—a show where I had drunk too much even before it started—but you could have been. It wasn't out of the realm of possibility. I'd show up somewhere and the bartender would be talking about you guys being there the night before. I did see you and Steve once, but it was out in Grand Prairie, the suburbs, at a Coldplay concert.

The band members (minus singer Chris Martin) came to your game against the Timberwolves the night before, and you met them after. You went home but Steve, of course, hit the town with them and hit it off, so he took you to the show. You went backstage and posed for photos with the group.

"It's just weird the stuff that happens, the people you meet," you told me. "Who would have thought that when I left Germany?"

I was there because I'd just written a cover story for the *Observer* on a band from out in Tyler called MossEisley (which soon, and smartly, changed its name to just Eisley) and they were opening for Coldplay and also *I like Coldplay*. You and Nash came in maybe a song or two into the set, at least after the lights were down, but you were hard to miss. You passed right in front of where we were sitting, scrunching down, ducking, moving into yourself like a fifteen-year-old would, not wanting to be seen, or wanting to let other people see, or both. I watched you watch Coldplay a little, and then you and Steve swiftly left just before the show wrapped up, capably working the two-man game off the court, too.

4

Every River That You Tried to Cross

Before the first game of your opening-round series against Portland in the 2003 playoffs, one of the coaches told you that you'd have to put the team on your back. You said: "Oh, I don't know if I can do that."

But you did. You scored forty-six points and pulled in ten rebounds in a win over the Trail Blazers, continuing your best season to that point.[13] After, Nellie said that you "will eventually be one of the best all-around players to ever play the game. He is just scratching the surface. His passing skills are just now starting to come out." Reality was finally catching up to his praise.

Scottie Pippen, then playing for the Blazers, said, "He learned a lot from me. Now I wish I'd learned from him." He went on to say—*Scottie Pippen*, your role model, said this—that you were "probably the only power forward I've seen that can do the things that he does out there—the ability to put the ball on the floor, the ability to shoot the ball from anywhere on the floor, the great court awareness."

---

13. Another level up: 25.1 points, with 9.9 boards and 3 assists a game.

You used all of that to lead the Mavs to a 3–0 lead in the series. You had forty-two points in Game 3, hitting fifteen of twenty shots, causing your teammate Nick Van Exel to say you shoot "threes where it looks like a layup. It's incredible to play with a seven-footer that strokes the ball so perfectly."

Then the Blazers became just the third team ever to force a Game 7 after losing the first three games in a series.

That, to some, served as a neat summation of your career: that you were an empty stat line, that you couldn't win the games that mattered. There was a molecule of truth there—you did turn in your only bad performance of the Portland series in Game 6, finishing with just four points—but you'd already proved it wrong time and again. And you did it in that series, closing out the Blazers two nights later with thirty-one and eleven, leading everyone on the court in both categories and all but ending your hero's career.[14]

Your biggest shot was a three with 1:21 left. Your arms went up and then around Van Exel, and then you caught Nash, who was jumping at you. It was a moment of triumph and relief and it reduced the prior three games to a minor annoyance, a slight plot complication.

Those three games, and your failure to lead your team to victory in any of them, would be held against you later.

⊕   ⊕   ⊕

14. Pippen would play just twenty-three games the next season with the Bulls, the final one on February 2, before retiring.

The Mavs' second-round series, a rematch against Sacramento, was one of the most satisfying basketball-watching experiences of my life, even removed from the context that you were trying to get revenge for being knocked out in the second round in 2002 by the Kings.

They won the first game and, after the narrow escape against Portland, let's say there was not a surplus of confidence in Dallas that 2003 would be any different than 2002. Then Game 2 happened. That is still how I think of it, no matter how many others could claim that title over the years:

GAME 2

It was like the basketball equivalent of hitting every greenlight for a thousand miles while at the wheel of a 1965 Ford GT40. It was soothing and thrilling at once, like playing with one of those perpetual motion toys while on the back of speeding fire engine. It was an overwhelmingly ecstatic event, a tent revival with a three-point line painted outside the pulpit; you guys might as well have been playing in choir robes. I was there, in the upper deck, in a corner, on such a steep incline I almost tumbled over the rows of seats high-fiving strangers during a first half that saw the Mavs score eighty-three points. Eighty-fucking-three motherfucking points. From up there, it looked like you all were throwing Ping-Pong balls into a swimming pool, especially Van Exel. You had an almost casual twenty and fourteen when it was over, and the next day I was so hoarse it

felt like a maintenance crew from the city had sandblasted graffiti off of my esophagus.

Game 2 was a watershed moment, the demons of the previous failures against the Kings exorcised, the sins of the previous round washed away. It was like a mini championship, something to hold on to when a real one didn't materialize later. But at that moment, I was convinced it was coming. It felt like you and the Mavs could and would defeat anyone. There were still five games to come in the series, not to mention two more potential rounds to get through in the playoffs, so it was probably too soon for all the euphoria. But I don't regret it. Not even a little.

The next game, you played all fifty-eight minutes of a double-overtime win, finishing with twenty-five points and twenty rebounds. Game 3 was more representative of the series, you making your presence felt more as a rebounder than on the offensive end, where the team was led by Van Exel. He only played a season and a half with you, but it's easy to see why you loved him so much; you told me in 2009 he was your favorite teammate. He didn't start a single game against Sacramento, but the lefty guard led the Mavs in scoring anyway, averaging 25.3 points while making twenty-four three-pointers, and even the numbers bely his impact. He gave Dallas some swagger—he was like if you made an entire human being out of self-confidence, shooting free throws a foot or so behind the line because he felt more at home farther back. I love Van Exel, too. He is my basketball Tyler Durden, a middle finger with a tight handle and a crooked smile, seemingly specifically designed to wear headbands at

a jaunty angle, the first (and, so far, only) Maverick to make it into a Jay-Z lyric.[15]

You said you had been "sleepwalking" through the series. But when it was time to close out the Kings, there you were, with thirty points and nineteen rebounds. "I wasn't a big factor the whole series," you said. "I couldn't find my rhythm. I'm glad my jumper was a little better than it was a couple days ago."

Game 7 of the series happened during an already-planned camping trip at Possum Kingdom Lake, a few hours west of Dallas, so my wife and I had to drive around the lake, shaped like the fallen corpse of a dragon, to find a place to watch it. It took almost an hour, and we ended up in the bar of a pretty nice restaurant at one of the lake's marinas. This was her first real exposure to basketball. I had gotten her hooked in March when my alma mater, the University of Texas Longhorns, led by guard T.J. Ford, made a run through the NCAA Tournament that ended in the Final Four. (They were knocked out by eventual champion Syracuse and its freshman star, Carmelo Anthony.) The NBA playoffs started soon after and, by then, she was invested enough that we took time out of a weekend trip to Houston to watch the first game of the Mavs-Blazers series, staying in our hotel room for most of a Saturday night.

We needed something to distract us, to pull us together, to get

---

15. "The ROC handle like Van Exel/I shake phonies, man, you can't get next to," from Beyoncé's debut solo single "Crazy in Love," in which she sings about how great Jay-Z is, and then Jay drops in to rap about . . . how great Jay-Z is. It was released in May 2003, so it's likely he recorded it during the Kings series.

us away from ourselves. A few months earlier—and, listen, I'm sorry for bringing this up here, but it's what happened—she had miscarried during her first trimester and it was crushing and when we found out it had been twins it was worse. Maybe I could just say "personal crisis" and keep it moving, or something else vague, but we all grew up together, right? We were shell-shocked for a few months, getting through the days but that's about it. We needed something to look forward to, a reason to keep moving beyond the fact that we had to. It turned out to be basketball, you and the Mavs, that finally did it. Not all heroes wear capes, etc. and so on.

And so, at the restaurant in the marina, overlooking the lake, we were the only ones there solely to watch the game, at least when it started. By the end, though, the bar was packed with onlookers, the mood rising and falling like the boats outside with each possession. It reflected what was happening back in Dallas, as you and the Mavericks, young and fun and on the rise, became the city's dominant sports team, finally.[16] I wasn't the only one who had found my way back.

It was, in its way, a bit like being at the game—celebrating with strangers, forming a community with a two-hour lifespan. It was exactly what we needed exactly when we needed it.

⊕ ⊕ ⊕

---

16. A position they'd hold until Tony Romo took over as the Cowboys' starting quarterback in the fall of 2006.

The "Big Three" era didn't officially end in the Western Conference finals against San Antonio. But we know that's just a technicality. Nash stayed for another season; Finley remained for two. It was different, though, after that series. What had been building since June 1998, when the Nelsons brought you and Nash in, within hours of each other, to team up with Finley—that was over, at least in that form.

Do you ever wonder what might have happened if you hadn't banged your left knee into Manu Ginobili while going for a rebound in the fourth quarter of the third game? That game was already decided, but what about everything that happened after? What if Nellie had let you try to come back, even if your knee wasn't 100 percent, in Game 4 (or 5 or 6)? What if the Mavs had been able to finish off their comeback without you?

You got lucky. That is the only thing anyone knows for sure. Dr. T. O. Souryal[17] said you were a few more degrees of hyperextension away from tearing an ACL or MCL, and that would have had you rehabbing into the next season. As it stood, you suffered a medial retinacular sprain, affecting the ligaments that hold the kneecap in place. The normal recovery time is ten to fourteen days. You tried to play two days later.

---

17. Dallas as small town: I ended up visiting Souryal in 2010 after hurting my knee running in the Dallas Marathon as part of a relay team. While having an X-ray taken of my knee, I looked over from the table I was lying on and saw a file containing your X-rays, alongside those of dozens of former Mavericks.

Nellie wouldn't hear of it. "I will not jeopardize his career at this point," he said before Game 4. "That would be pretty silly. When he came to the U.S., his father told me that I'm his father in America. He's his father in Germany. And as his father in America, he will not play." He said you wouldn't take the court until your knee was "perfect," that you'd "crawl out there" if you could, but it was not your decision.

Unfortunately, outside of Dallas, this went on your permanent record as a failure on your part. In 2009's *The Book of Basketball*, Bill Simmons, the former ESPN columnist, NBA analyst, and founder of The Ringer, wrote, "The 'soft' tag started in '03 when Dirk refused to limp around with an injured knee in the '03 conference finals. Strangely, no one remembers this now." While none of this section on Dirk aged particularly well, I'm not picking on Simmons—this was fairly representative of how people viewed you. Maybe I am picking on him a little bit.

Regardless of what other people said, or even what you thought, you had to admit Nellie's decision was the correct one. "Even just standing up during the game, I could feel that my knee wasn't right," you told me in 2009.

You kept trying anyway—*Dirk would crawl out there*. You worked up a sweat before Games 4, 5, and 6, showing Nellie and Cuban how you could move. Cuban wanted you to play. "I think that's where it started, where they went their separate ways," you said to me. "After that, years later, obviously, it got very ugly. But that's the first time they weren't agreeing on some stuff."

Nellie held firm and saved you from yourself, and maybe saved

the franchise in the process. What if you came out in Game 4 or 5 and landed on that knee the wrong way, or stepped on someone's foot (longtime irritant Bruce Bowen was still on the Spurs, after all), got tangled up on a screen? Or planted too hard changing directions? The Mavs still lose to the Spurs, and maybe they were always going to; the Spurs won the title that year. But now they lose you, too, not just for a series but maybe longer. Maybe forever. Maybe you're never the same after that. Once injuries start, there's not always a path back for some players. Grant Hill was able to have a few productive seasons as a role player before he retired. Penny Hardaway wasn't. Brandon Roy retired in what should have been his prime.

You didn't have to look far to see. The 2003 playoffs had already altered the trajectory of one player's career—and, with it, the future of a franchise—when Chris Webber tore cartilage in a left knee that had been bothering him all season. You were there. It happened in the first half of Game 2 against Sacramento. Initially, the repair of Webber's lateral meniscus was supposed to only keep him out for four to six weeks, after arthroscopic surgery. But he ended up requiring the much more serious, much riskier microfracture procedure and missed all but the final twenty-three games of the 2003–04 season. Webber managed to put up decent numbers for a few more years, but he never regained the athleticism that made him special. He couldn't move side to side, couldn't jump. He still saw the game like few others; his body couldn't keep up. He retired after playing only nine games in the 2007–08 season, but his career had largely been over long before. Maybe since Game 2.

The Kings still had Peja Stojaković and Mike Bibby and added outdoors enthusiast Brad Miller to their frontcourt. They'd beat the Mavs again in the playoffs. But their title window very definitely started to close when Webber went down. "We were so close so many times," former Kings co-owner Joe Maloof said in 2008, when Webber announced his retirement. "But after that injury, that's when the gradual decline of that particular group we put together started. We never really recovered."

The team traded Webber and Doug Christie in 2005 and Stojaković a year later. They still made the playoffs in 2005–06, barely, as the eighth seed, but haven't been back since, which, as of this writing, is fourteen seasons and counting.

That could have been you. That could have been the Mavericks. That *had* been the Mavericks at the outset of the 1990s, when their roster was a Jenga tower built on the foundation of Roy Tarpley's fragile sobriety. If you had seriously injured yourself against the Spurs, the team might have plunged right back into the quicksand of NBA mediocrity, only a couple of years after it had managed to extract itself. Very rarely does anyone get to see the road not taken, the other side of the sliding doors—the ligament not torn—quite as clearly as the Mavs did in 2003.

But, OK, as long as we are doing this: what if you hadn't gotten injured at all?

Given that the Mavs' roster was deep enough that they almost forced a Game 7 even without you following Game 3, I think you would have carried them to the Finals, and I think you would have

defeated the New Jersey Nets, just as the Spurs did. I'm not saying that only as a fan of the Mavs or you or counterfactual histories, though, obviously, I am very much all three. The Spurs weren't *the Spurs* yet in 2003. Tim Duncan was in his prime (and he really pretty much always was), but Tony Parker was twenty years old and in his second season. Ginobili was a rookie—albeit one who was twenty-five and coming off massive success in Europe—who people still called Emanuel. Former Dream Teamer David Robminson was thirty-seven, had a bad back, and was a few weeks away from retirement. They were giving rotation minutes to a forty-year-old Kevin Willis. The Spurs were good but had room to improve, and they weren't better than the Mavs in 2003, not really, not when you were out there.

So, you don't get hurt, you and Nash win a title together, the "Big Three" win a title together, and maybe that era is allowed to continue, to come to a rest on its own momentum, not taken apart piece by piece. Maybe then Cuban listens to Nellie and decides it's worth re-signing Nash instead of letting him go to Phoenix. As you said, the fallout from your knee injury led to a rift between Cuban and Nelson, and that probably affected Nash's departure, since Nellie reportedly very strongly advocated to retain him. And Nash leaving led to Nelson admittedly losing interest in the team, which led to him handing over head coaching duties to his assistant (and former point guard) Avery Johnson, and Johnson being in charge led to his changing the starting lineup of a sixty-seven-win team in the 2007 playoffs, thinking that he could outsmart

his former boss, which led to me knowing, with absolute certainty, that the Mavs were absolutely fucked against Nellie and the "We Believe" Warriors as soon as I heard the PA announcer say "Devean George" while sitting in Section 319 for Game 1. Am I arguing that your knee injury cost the Mavs titles in 2003 and 2007? Yes, and I'm sure I could make a case for 2005 and 2006, too. 2004 was doomed by the garbage-bag uniforms you wore in the first game of the season, a blowout loss to the Lakers, and Antoine Walker, in that order. We'll get there.

With no Nash, Phoenix's "Seven Seconds or Less" era is over before it begins, losing the point guard who made it all work. And with Nash still around, maybe you don't get as good as you eventually became, without having to take over a team, to make it yours, to shoulder the load on your own. If Steve and Mike don't leave, you can still do what comes naturally and pull them into the frame with you. And with that lack of pressure, with no crucible to forge you, maybe you don't quite get there. You're a great player but not an all-timer. You're LaMarcus Aldridge or Pau Gasol. No MVP trophy, no ascent to that next level of stardom.

It probably worked out best for everyone. Even Nellie looks fantastic now, tan and trim, living in Hawaii, growing and smoking pot and playing poker with Willie Nelson.

⊕　⊕　⊕

I watched the final game of the Mavs' 2002–03 season in a large,

creaky rental house in East Dallas surrounded by the most casual front-running Spurs fans imaginable, transplants who had moved north a few years earlier and seemed to care about the Spurs only as a screw-you to their adopted hometown. I suppose it was my punishment for allowing my support to waver and my fandom to wander in the mid-to-late 1990s. I didn't deserve to come back only when the team's fortunes had improved and completely avoid any repercussions. I had to remember that it could hurt again. I had to let it. Only after I had shed every last trace of cynicism and shut down all my self-defense mechanisms would I be ready, baptized anew. *You have to die if you want to be alive.* My man Jeff Tweedy said that, right around this time. I died on Miller Street, the same night you and the Mavs did.

In Game 6, an incredibly entertaining roster[18] pushed the Spurs right to the brink of a Game 7. They were up thirteen points with 10:53 remaining.

They ended up losing by twelve.

Have you thought about this much since then? I have. On the road and out of options, Spurs coach Gregg Popovich brought in guard Steve Kerr—thirty-seven and in his last season in the league—to change the energy. Really, just to save his other guards' legs for the forthcoming Game 7. Kerr only played in ten of a possible twenty-four

---

18. Aside from you, Nash, and Finley, as well as Van Exel, there were guys like Raja Bell, Walt Williams, Adrian Griffin, and Eddie Najera—players who knew exactly what their role was and never tried to do more or ever did less.

games during the Spurs' playoff run. Prior to that appearance, he had played a total of two minutes and nine seconds for the entire series.

And then

And   then

And   then

And

then

And

then

And

then

And

then

And then, while I was surrounded by cackling Spurs

fans—including one woman, my wife's ex-roommate, who was watching her first game of the season—Kerr came in walk-in-freezer cold and hit four three-pointers, leading the Spurs on a game-deciding, series-ending 23–0 run. It was like Al Capone getting busted on tax evasion that it was Kerr to do it, not Duncan or Parker or Ginobili or almost literally anyone else. He ripped out the collective heart of the Mavs and their fans, paraded it around the arena on the end of a pike, then flamboyantly set it ablaze, scooped up the ashes, loaded them into the nose cone of a nuclear missile, fired it at the moon, changing its orbit and causing the Earth's oceans to rise and swallow us whole, making way for a new society led by dolphins.

Maybe I'm not completely over it yet.

⊕   ⊕   ⊕

The most famous or infamous or let's just say well-known instance of you and Steve out on the town happened soon after. You remember. You were at Woody's Tavern in Fort Worth, a week after the Spurs knocked you guys out. I can't imagine what would have happened if Twitter had been around then. My god. I mean, people were *emailing* the resulting photos—featuring the two of you, at least a couple of beers in, and some random doughy frat kid—to each other, which sounds as ancient now as if they had actually printed them out and put them in envelopes and stamped them and taken them to the post office. They ended up in my inbox a handful of times.

I could probably paint these photos from memory, I've seen

them so much. The frat guy's cherubic, Bud Light-and-baby fat cheeks and chin-only Shaggy-Doo goatee. Nash's pre-Bieber shag and mouth hanging open like an overhead bin prior to takeoff. *Your* chin-only goatee and eyes on power-save mode, backward hat and hint of gold hoop earring. The kid's red-and-tan checkered shirt. Nash looking like a duckface selfie had somehow traveled a decade back in time. To me, these are the defining images of the "Dirk and Steve" era, even though they came near the end, because they aren't of two teammates. They are of two friends.

Nash doesn't regret it: "Will they go away? I hope not. Classic," he told me once when I asked him about the photos.[19] I know you don't either. But maybe you regret the goatee a little bit?

---

19. "It was a regular night," Nash said. "The only thing that made it different is that someone had a camera."

5

As Soon As You Give It All Up You Can Have It All

Most likely caught up in the emotion of that playoff run, my wife and I bought a half-season ticket package before the 2003–04 season, a pair of seats in a corner of the upper deck, Section 319. We got half of the forty-one home games and every other playoff game. It was a pretty good deal that we could just barely afford.

Seated next to us were two guys who would become our best friends in the world, but only at Mavs games. I'll call them Lando and Han. It took us most of that first season to learn their actual names. Lando was Black and always wore a Mavs visor and a blue Michael Finley jersey (he'd switch to a No. 5 Josh Howard at the end of the following season). He talked shit incessantly and sang along with whatever came over the PA during timeouts. Han was white and always dressed like he'd just gotten off work, mostly because he'd always just gotten off work. He was a close talker after he'd had a few beers, even more so if he and Lando had a chance to hit the downstairs Old No. 7 Club pregame. Lando and Han had a standing over-under bet on how long it would take Shawn Bradley to fall down awkwardly once he checked into a game. They were lively and fun game-watching company.

But the 2003–04 season was a bit of a comedown. It all went backward: from sixty wins to fifty-two; from the Western Conference finals to a five-game loss to the Kings in the first round. Your numbers went down, too, forced to play center all year and having to give up shots to new teammates. Mostly, it just wasn't as fun. Nick Van Exel was traded to Golden State for Antawn Jamison (and future coach Avery Johnson), and as much as I hated to lose Van Exel, that would have been fine. Jamison was bigger, five years younger, and adding his off-kilter game of flips and scoops and push shots to you and Nash and Finley was like inserting a knuckleball pitcher into the starting rotation, a dimension that would keep defenses constantly on their heels. Van Exel's shooting created one kind of space. This might have created another. But no one knows if it actually would have worked, because just over a week before the season started, the Mavs also traded for Antoine Walker, and he got in everyone's way. At best, it would have been a redundant move even if Walker and Jamison didn't share a first name (at least in pronunciation).

Walker was a former All-Star for the Boston Celtics, a big playmaking power forward who loved to shoot threes. (He was the guy who famously answered, after someone asked why he shot so many, "Because there are no fours.") I doubt you'd say anything bad about his brief time here, so let me: he took the ball out of Nash's hands, made you play out of position, took shots from everyone, and made everything feel harder than it needed to be. Other than that, he was fine. I would guess that a third of his rebounds came from his own missed layups, and he played with the same expression on his face

I would have if an ex-girlfriend showed up at the concert I was at, to pick a completely arbitrary comparison that definitely never happened.

It wasn't bad. There was simply too much talent for the team to be *bad*. But it wasn't good, either. Maybe it's just my memory making it worse, but it all felt like such a struggle, like nothing was working out the way everyone thought it would.

The first game of the season set the tone. You remember. It's probably the one thing everyone remembers about that season. The Mavs played the Lakers at the Staples Center in L.A., in a nationally televised game on TNT, and the team debuted new uniforms. I guess "debut" is not the right word, because it implies they would be seen again. I'm honestly not sure that the equipment manager, your buddy Al Whitley, brought them back from Los Angeles. They weren't the worst jerseys in the world, but you guys didn't look good in them. They were an alternate take on your normal road blues, but with a base color that couldn't quite decide if it wanted to be gray or silver. It was too shiny for the former, too dark for the latter, and the fabric didn't look like it was meant to be worn, or maybe even seen, absolutely not under arena lighting. On TV, they looked slick—and I'm not the first person to make this comparison—like garbage bags.[20] And when they got sweaty, the jerseys didn't look silver or gray but more of a murky brown, like they should be on a rack at REI, worn

---

20. You *were* in L.A., so maybe we can say it was a tribute to the Go-Go's, who wore dresses made of garbage bags when they were starting out.

around a campfire while wearing toe shoes, some earth-tone, flannel-tied-around-your-waist business. Mark Cuban probably decided they would never be worn again after the first quarter.

From the start, it was one of those times when it felt like the other team was playing Pop-a-Shot while the Mavs were shooting on a twelve-foot rim with a medicine ball. In Dallas, you could almost feel that every fan had stopped caring about winning and had turned all of their energy to achieving a respectable loss. Not being a joke.

It always seemed to be the Lakers, the fucking *Lakers*, the *fucking* Lakers, who were the opponent in these situations. The Mavericks' constant failure to live up to the Lakers mirrored the city of Dallas's yearning to be seen as equals to L.A. (or New York or Chicago or, I mean, even to Austin or Houston). (Covering music, I'd seen how rappers had to compete with Houston's better-known scene, and everyone else had to deal with Austin and its only partially earned mythic status.) We'd swear to people who weren't paying attention that the Mavs were great, that Dallas was great, and then a nationally televised Lakers game would happen, some embarrassing news story would pop up, and everyone would consider the city and the team the same as ever. We couldn't win. The strides were made in secret, but the slip-ups occurred under a spotlight under a microscope.

The Lakers were debuting their own offseason acquisitions (and future Hall of Famers) Gary Payton and Karl Malone, but the team was without superstar guard Kobe Bryant, rehabbing from knee surgery. They still scored the first eight points of the game and led

29–15 after the first quarter, and it felt much worse than that. Walker (nineteen points and 5-6 from three) and Jamison (seventeen points off the bench) played well, but you (nineteen points on 5-17 shooting), Nash (eight points, 7 assists), and Finley (twelve points, mostly on free throws) did not. Like the new uniforms, it was already clear that the roster was less than the sum of its parts, a collection of decent decisions that turned into one overarching bad one. They were both sort of laboratory creations that didn't hold up in real-world conditions. That's the way it goes, sometimes: you can't know you're going to fuck something up until you fuck it up. I've done that to cars, magazine features, a marriage. Again: you have to learn how to die if you want to be alive.

But the Mavs couldn't just get rid of a problematic roster as easily as the Hefty-brand jerseys. That would have to wait until the next summer.

⊕   ⊕   ⊕

Do you remember anything else about that forgettable season? I remember one other game, for obvious reasons. It's not because it was the first time that LeBron James visited Dallas in his professional career, although that was remarkable. It's because it was the night my son was almost born at a Mavs game.

It didn't come all that close, really, but it's a better way of telling the story.

March 30 was Isaac's due date and I had planned to be at home,

waiting, as I had been for weeks. Instead, I was at a Mavericks game with my friend Eric, like I was trying to get a head start on being a deadbeat dad.

The sales director at the *Observer* had given me the company's tickets, which usually went to clients, a prime pair on the first row of the Platinum section at the AAC. I couldn't have afforded them if the Timberwolves had been in town, much less LeBron. The sales director didn't do this because he liked me, particularly, although we were friendly enough. He just liked chaos. What he wanted was for me to take my incredibly pregnant wife to the game, with the hope that, at some point, she would go into labor. Once he gave me the tickets, if I'm being honest, that's kind of what I was hoping, too. I wish that weren't true. I wish I still didn't hope that it had happened that way.

But, anyway, she wouldn't come with me and didn't even really consider it. I still can't figure out why she insisted I go, although a couple of months earlier, already extremely pregnant, she had also insisted on painting the entire bathroom, including the ceiling, a deep ocean blue, and insisted on doing it herself. So her decision-making after her sixth month of pregnancy was unpredictable, to say the least. She was unpredictable in general and adding pregnancy to the mix was like living with a roulette wheel. I guess that's why I thought, for a moment, that she would take the tickets.

She did go into labor that night, right around the time the game was ending. I rushed home—and then we waited. Isaac was born two days later, early in the morning on April 1, a long-running April Fool's Day prank. And maybe being born at a Mavs game, with

LeBron James in attendance, was a bit too much weight to put on Isaac's shoulders. What if he wasn't good at basketball? What if he didn't like it? What if he grew up to resent me? It wasn't like I would have named him LeBron. I probably would have named him after you. Maybe just his middle name. After all, he was born on 4/1.

As for the game: you had thirty-five and eighteen and the win took the Mavs to 46–28 on the season. LeBron had twenty-eight points and watching him play was like walking into the Sistine Chapel while Michelangelo was halfway through with the ceiling.

⊕   ⊕   ⊕

It was probably for the best that there would be no extended play-off run in 2004, that the season would end after five disappointing games against Sacramento. For me it was probably for the best, I mean. When the Mavs lost by one on the road, despite your thirty-one points and fourteen rebounds, Isaac was twenty-nine days old. I don't think I slept through a full night for another few months. I'm not sure I could have physically withstood losing sleep over basketball, too. Back then, I'd have trouble going to sleep after a Wednesday night game in February, if I thought you should have won, and I always thought you should have won.

But you almost kept it going against the Kings. The Mavs were within one because you'd gotten an offensive rebound with just under thirty seconds left and scored, then blocked Mike Bibby's short jumper to give yourself one more chance. But your fifteen-footer at

the buzzer wouldn't fall, and that was it. It was over—the season and your time spent playing with Steve.

"We talked about it," you told me a few years later. "I didn't think it was going to happen . . . We made it this far, we thought for sure, you know, we were going to end our careers together. That's how we were talking. That's how great we were fitting together and gelling together. Steve, it just came as a shock more than anything. We knew there was the possibility that somebody might try and sign him, but we never thought it would happen."

Cuban had already paid you and Finley, giving you both around $100 million. And he was known for spending whatever it took to win. So when he was hesitant to sign Steve to an extension before he hit free agency, everyone probably should have been more concerned than they were. But I guess no one thought that the two of you would be separated, that you could be. You were a package deal, on and off the court, from the very beginning, from the day when you were both introduced to Dallas in twin ridiculous hairstyles. Until 2004, you were always thought of together, Dirk and Nash. Even on the poster for *Like Mike* you were together. It was like you were running a pick and roll through life.

And then in the draft in June, the team traded Jamison to the Washington Wizards for Jerry Stackhouse and the No. 5 pick, which they used on Devin Harris, a point guard out of Wisconsin. Did you start to think then that Steve might not be coming back? Because I did.

But Steve would have stayed if the Mavs had matched the

Phoenix Suns' offer, and maybe their enthusiasm, too. They showed up as early as possible to recruit him, a big contingent including coach Mike D'Antoni and star Amar'e Stoudemire, and presented him with a plan for an up-tempo offense that would play to his strengths, that they believed he was the only player who could truly make work, and a contract worth $63 million over six years. Steve took it back to Cuban to see if he would match; the previous offer had been for four years, with a fifth only partially guaranteed, for $9 million per season. Cuban said no.

Steve called you and you told him that if it was that much more money, then he had to do it. He had twins on the way, a new family to look after. He called again after he signed with the Suns, and you backed him up again, saying that he had made the right decision. You were the first call he made.

"I guess that shows how close we really were," you told me, and still now, seeing that past tense *were*, it picks at a scab, opens an old wound, brings to mind that alternate path—whether 2006 and 2007 would have been different, whether you still would be you, how it all might have changed, for better and worse. Would you have become the player you were if you didn't have to do it alone? Would Dallas have gotten to see the real you if you could have continued to hide behind Steve?

But more than any of that, that *were* reminds me that two friends had to be split apart and that their relationship was made to suffer and wither a bit, that the NBA, at least for a while, turned two brothers into college roommates, connected but distant, sharing a past but

not much of a present. Players are all forced, at some point, to view the league as a business. Fans are even more compartmentalized, hating players until they end up on their teams, *our* teams, loving them until they leave, treating them as numbers—stats or contracts or both, pieces to be rearranged on a board. We see them as teammates but rarely as friends, tossing out the players' emotions to make room for our own. That *were* makes me sad for me, too.

⊕   ⊕   ⊕

But at the time, in late June 2004, I was more worried that *you* wouldn't be coming back.

The Lakers had lost in the Finals against the Detroit Pistons, and the simmering feud between Kobe Bryant and Shaquille O'Neal boiled over. It quickly became obvious that one of them would have to leave and just about as quickly that the one who would be leaving was Shaq. And where was he going?

"Right now, I'd love to go to Dallas," Shaq's then-wife Shaunie told *EXTRA!* "Love to go! Hint, hint—so, Mark, if you're listening . . ."

First off, no one *ever* wanted to go to Dallas, to play on the Mavs or do much of anything, so that was kind of exhilarating and strange and took more than a little getting used to. After it stopped feeling like a prank, a way to get our hopes up just so it would feel worse when it inevitably didn't happen, the idea of pairing you and Shaq, the best center of his generation and one of the best of all time, two gravitational forces whose mere presence on the court shifted the orbit of a defense,

it was almost too much to comprehend, like hearing God's voice. (You'd assume it's comfortable and confident, like Morgan Freeman or maybe Sam Elliott, but it's probably more like the roar of a thousand lions in the middle of a swarm of locusts on fire.) The rest of the roster didn't really matter; you two would be enough. It didn't guarantee a championship, of course—the most recent Finals had proved that much—but it would have put the Mavs on that level for the next few seasons. It raised the floor. No more first-round exits.

Lost in that excitement was the simple truth that there was no way the Lakers would trade Shaq to Dallas without getting you back in return. Did you think Cuban was going to send you to L.A.? Did you imagine what it would be like to play with Kobe? You would have been fascinating teammates, two insanely hard workers whose games fit together like Velcro, a devastating two-man game, a crunchtime duo with no real weakness. He wanted to be The Man and you would be happy to let him. You could play that part, too, but you didn't *need* it. Kobe won two championships with Pau Gasol—an obviously great player, but a B-plus version of you. Think of what would have happened if he'd had access to the genuine article, and in your prime.

Cuban knew what he had in you and didn't waver. There was only one Shaq, he said. There was also only one Dirk Nowitzki. And so, on July 14, Shaq was traded to Miami instead. By then, Nash was already gone, too.

⊕   ⊕   ⊕

After Nash left, the Mavs—always good at coming up with a backup plan—traded Antoine Walker to the Atlanta Hawks in exchange for Jason Terry, better known as Jet, a shooting guard in a point guard's body. I didn't know much about him, other than he had poured in forty-six points during a game against you guys in 2002.

(And, in fact, until just this moment when I looked it up, I always remembered it as him going for fifty points, putting him in the random group of players who had aberrant career nights against us. Like Andre Miller—then with Portland and known more for throwing perfect lob passes and being built like a half-filled backpack than for his prowess as a scorer—who went for fifty-two points, with only one (!) three-pointer. Isn't it funny how memory does that? Until I went to Terry's Basketball Reference page, I was *certain*, dead sure, that he had scored fifty points against the Mavs. I even remembered where I was when the game happened—half watching on the bar TV at some fast-casual joint—and could vaguely recall the *SportsCenter* highlight package and the newspaper recap, and it didn't exist. It was a movie quote that I slightly reworded and then repeated and repeated, the edited version rewritten over the original.)

I don't know about you, but I was happy to be done with Walker, and Jet seemed to be a better immediate replacement for Nash, especially on a team with title aspirations, than rookie Devin Harris. Also, with his bottomless confidence, his crooked headband and tall socks, his insouciant style, and even his No. 31 jersey, it was like they had recast the part of Nick Van Exel, brought us a new Aunt Viv halfway through the show. So it was easy to see him as more than a credible

substitute for Nash on the court, different but still effective in his own way. But, again, that wasn't exactly what he was meant to fill in for, and everyone knew it, and you most especially. He had an impossible job. Did you tell him that? Did anyone? Did anyone have to?

Even if it was just on the court, Terry had too much to live up to. With the Suns, Steve was flourishing, reaching the sort of heights the two of you had dreamed of, two gym rats working to be the best, pushing each other, trying to get the most out of what you'd been given, to rise to the top of the sport. It was supposed to happen together. But you were in Dallas and he was in Phoenix on his way to back-to-back MVP trophies.

It's strange to say, since you were twenty-six years old then, but you finally had to grow up, in a way, when Steve left. It was time to take over the family business, time to take on the face-of-the-franchise duties you'd been able to avoid or dilute for so long, sharing them with Nash and Finley when you couldn't disappear completely. I'm talking mostly about off-the-court responsibilities, but it carried over. You were now the focal point of a more conventional team, with an actual center, albeit one, in Erick Dampier, with frying-pan hands and modest production. And you took to the role quickly. On December 2, you scored forty-three points in regulation and fifty-three for the game—ten straight in overtime—in a win over the Rockets, a duel with Tracy McGrady, who had forty-eight of his own. "This was like Jordan and Bird hooking up," a giddy Jet said. "This will be on ESPN Classic." You finished the season with your highest scoring average so far, 26.1 per game. By the end, you'd also be playing under a more conventional

coach, who would soon push you to be a more conventional player. Don Nelson, your American father, left and your former teammate, Avery Johnson, less than a year removed from his playing days, took over, heading up the last eighteen games and going 16–2.

Eras were ending all over—Finley was almost gone, too. He would be in San Antonio, of all places, when the 2005 season began. It's worth taking a moment to note that your steady presence gave the organization the illusion of continuity, but that's not really true, is it? When you look at twenty-one seasons of rosters in one sitting, there is a wild amount of turnover. Players come and go, some come back, but there aren't many constants.

After Nash and Finley, your most rewarding and lengthy partnership was with Jet. You've talked about how you and he "bonded right away from day one," and you fell into a two-man game with him as comfortably as if you'd been on the same AAU squad together. And he stepped up in the first-round series against Houston, when you struggled with your shot[21] and the Mavs lost the first two games, both at home. Jet shot 60 percent from behind the arc and upped his scoring to eighteen a game.

(I was at the second game of the Rockets series, in which Tracy McGrady threw down a dunk that was war-movie violent, ending with him riding on Shawn Bradley's back like the seven-foot-six center was a pony at a kid's birthday. And I was at Game 7, in which the tension that had built up dissolved into a forty-point Mavs win

---

21. A rough 35 percent from the floor and 28 percent from three.

that wasn't actually even that close and wiped away all that had come before. The only remaining artifact is McGrady's dunk on Bradley, which may have legitimately ended the giant Mormon's career. He played one second in the next game, and just fifteen minutes over the rest of the postseason, almost all in deep garbage time.)

But your first season with Terry, and first without Nash, wasn't always easy and it didn't end easily, with a mostly one-sided shouting match in front of a home playoff crowd and a national TV audience serving as the final flicker of life, you raging against the dying of the light, and an inexplicable defensive miscue. The Mavs were up three in the second round against Nash and the Suns, about to force a series-deciding Game 7. Time was running out, Nash had the ball, everyone knew the Suns needed a three-pointer, everyone *everyone* knew that Nash was the Sun's best shooter—and Jet backed off, giving him an open shot that went through the net as time expired, sending the game into overtime. They might as well have called it right then.

You, understandably, lost your shit, screaming at Terry right there in front of everyone. I felt queasy watching you explode—one of the only times I've seen pure anger on your face, something coming from a deeper place than an argument over a blown foul call—the kind of nausea you feel in your feet and shoulders, like your blood wants to throw up. Your words hit Jet and all who saw with the sting of a slap, the aftermath somehow worse than what brought it on. And it felt, for a moment, like you and Jet might not come back from it. But you did, even though smaller eruptions would always be part of your dynamic. Terry told me in 2009 that the two of you got over it

by working out together, going out to dinner, finding your version of the relationship you had with Steve, becoming more than teammates but not quite best friends.

The game against the Suns was the close of the first chapter of a story that—several years later and with a ton more heartbreak in between—would again bring you and Jet together on the court, in front of a playoff crowd in Miami and everyone watching around the world. But then the two of you would be hugging tenderly, you cradling the back of his head as he leaned against your shoulder. Your expressions were almost more of relief than delight, all the ups and downs (and downs and downs and downs) playing across your faces. But that seemed a long way off in 2005, almost impossible to conjure.

And it almost *had* to be Steve that ended the season for you and Jet, that caused all of that, didn't it? I think more than any other professional sports league, the NBA runs on narrative, with tiny personal arcs and broad, epic themes routinely surfacing in its biggest moments. It's difficult to think of a Finals that didn't have a storyline, an easy sell, a natural hook. They're all parables; there's almost always a moral. So, yes, it *had* to be Steve that came back to Dallas to run you through with his sword, to conquer the land that had sent him into exile. His first season away, your first season apart, could not end any other way. That series[22] could not have ended any other

---

22. Which saw him average thirty points, twelve assists, and almost seven rebounds, and included one game in which he had forty-eight points and another where he had twenty-seven points and seventeen assists.

way. The finish to Game 6 happened as soon as he signed his name on the contract with Phoenix, it just took the better part of a year for it to show up in our timeline.

Just as assuredly, once Game 6 happened, then the 2006 Western Conference finals was set into motion, a return ticket printed and waiting to be picked up at the will call window. Because there was no way you and Nash's story would end like that. Not since we are telling it from your perspective. Maybe it would be different in *I See You, Little Canadian*.

⊕   ⊕   ⊕

In 2009, I asked Steve if he thought the two of you would have won a championship together if he hadn't left, if Dallas and Cuban had matched Phoenix's offer.

"Of course," he said. "Why not? I mean, you never know. Keeping me in Dallas wouldn't have really affected their salary cap situation. They still would have been able to bring in the other guys they brought in, for the most part. I think it would have been interesting. But that will all be barstool debate when we're long done playing."

It's difficult not to wonder and harder still to disagree with him. And while it would have been nice, and deserved, if you *had* gotten there with each other, no one remembers your time together in Dallas as a failure. You achieved something else, and maybe something better.

"I think the times you remember are the times away from the game—on the bus, the plane, the locker room," Nash told me. "In Dirk and I's case, you know, going out to dinner on the road, or even in Dallas. Neither one of us were much for cooking. Those memories, and the laughs, and the friends we had in common, those are the things you remember. I remember that, one, how much fun it was to kind of grow up in the NBA, so to speak. You know, we went from being on the worst team, unheralded, to being one of the top teams and respected. And, two, the fact that I got to know all of his friends and family, and he got to know all of mine. That everyone got to share all of that together."

The two of you rescued professional basketball in Dallas together. Michael Finley's contributions can't be overlooked, but it was you and Steve's relationship that captured the public's imagination, here and everywhere else. There was no real success to show for it, no trophies, at least, no championships or Finals appearances, not even much in the way of personal achievement. But just bringing the Mavericks back to any kind of relevance, given where they had been, was its own reward.

You'd have to keep going on your own, but those years with Steve helped prepare you for his absence. They made sure that you could.

6

We Could Open Up
Our Hearts and Fall In

Sometime in early 2006, I decided to run for mayor of Dallas. I can't give you credit (or blame) for this decision: I was a thirty-one-year-old magazine editor, with zero political experience and not even a ton of name recognition in my chosen field. Bands I had given bad reviews to, they knew me. But you did make Dallas somewhere I wanted to be, to stay. So it is a little bit your fault.

I hadn't planned to live in Dallas forever. It made the most sense after I graduated from the University of Texas—I had already had a summer internship at the *Observer*—but I saw it as the logical next step to the *next* step, wherever that might be. I considered Chicago, Nashville, a few other places. But after a couple of years in Dallas, I got married, and a few years after that, my son was born, and somewhere in there, we bought a house. Suddenly, I had roots, a young family, and a thirty-year mortgage. I quit the *Observer* in 2005, a year after Isaac was born, and spent a couple of years working for American Airlines' in-flight magazine, which gave me more free time than I was used to. (My editor wondered why I wanted to write at all, instead of just assigning stories to other writers.) That

provided me the opportunity to reflect on my life for the first time since I moved to Dallas, to take stock of my situation and start looking toward the future. I realized, as imperfect as it was and is, that I loved Dallas, enough that I wanted to fix it. Maybe that's something you've thought about before, too.

I doubt I can properly explain why I thought it should be me that could or would or should fix it, or why I thought I had a shot at getting the job. But I can tell you why I wanted to be mayor and why I thought I should run. Why I loved Dallas. And part of that was that you seemed to love Dallas, that you stayed here, were making your own home here. If you could come all the way from Germany and find your place in Dallas, then I could drive an hour up I-35. You didn't use Dallas as just a step along the way, a section on your Wikipedia page, the beginning of something. By staying, you'd rescued the Mavericks and you'd maybe helped rescue the city a little bit in the process.

I wouldn't get the same chance to do my part. We'll get to that.

⊕　⊕　⊕

When I say you rescued the Mavericks, I'm usually speaking broadly about pulling the franchise back from the brink. But I mean specific moments, too.

Has anyone ever told you what they did at the end of that Spurs game in 2006, the seventh and final game of the Western Conference semifinals, how they handled the stress? Did any of them lock one of their friends outside? We did.

Joe had left the house as soon as Manu Ginobili's inevitable shot put the Spurs up three, capping their comeback and pretty literally feeling like a dagger. We could see him through the sliding glass door, power-smoking a cigarette, pacing, mourning another almost. There were 32.9 seconds left in a game the Mavs should have won, in a series that should have already been over. It shouldn't have come to this. You know. The Mavs had been up twenty with 3:15 left in the second quarter and fourteen at the half. It felt like it should have been more: the team had made fifteen of seventeen shots at one point. Plus, you, *oh man*, you had it all working—off the dribble, the free-throw-line post-ups, elbow fadeaways. Your passing was crisp. You were rebounding and playing defense. Then the Spurs started chipping away.

The team had a 3–1 lead and had stolen homecourt advantage, and it felt like it was finally time. But the series had played out like that last game. Like the entire decade. The Spurs were the Mavs' nemesis, the constant thorn in their paw. This version of the Spurs had coalesced the year before you joined the league, and they had routinely showed up to inform you that you weren't ready yet. It was the Spurs that had ended your first trip to the playoffs, leaving you bloody-mouthed and with a jack-o'-lantern smile for your trouble. It had been the Spurs that caught up to you guys in 2003, ensuring that the franchise's best season in its history—the first time the Mavs had won sixty games, you leading the way with career highs across the board—wouldn't be enough to earn the top seed going into the postseason. And they had ended *that* playoff run, too, when you injured your knee and Steve Kerr's right arm turned into a flamethrower.

In 2006, of course, *of course*, they were again there to play the safe, steady tortoise to Dallas's flashy hare, the river creating a canyon, as consistent and clear-cut as their black-and-white color scheme. The Spurs were like if the classic scene in every horror movie—the one where the hero thinks he has finally vanquished the killer and turns his back for a few seconds and when he turns back around the body has vanished from the floor—could play basketball.

There were ghosts from 2003 all over this final game. Michael Finley and Nick Van Exel were on the Spurs' roster, which couldn't have felt great for you, and Kerr was there, too, calling the game for TNT, a fucking black cat sitting on the sideline, my god. For your part, you were showing what might have been back then, if you could have played or Nellie had let you.[23] None of it was going to matter. There was probably at least a small part of you, a tickle in your brain, that wanted to go outside the SBC Center when Ginobili's shot fell through the net, and surely a part of that part wanted to power-smoke like Joe.

but wait

What happened next was the kind of sequence, the type of shot

---

23. You had twenty points and fourteen rebounds in Game 1, then twenty-one and nine, twenty-seven and fifteen (including twenty-one of twenty-four from the free-throw line), twenty-eight and nine in almost the full forty-eight minutes, thirty-one and ten, and twenty-six and twenty-one in Game 6, where you missed a tying three with six seconds left.

that traditionally happened *to* the Mavs and *to* you. It rarely went in your favor. Just the season before, there had been Nash's open three-pointer that led to your argument with Jet and the ignominious end to another season. It was the kind of thing that I thought had already happened on that night, when Ginobili scored. That's why Joe was outside.

but wait

You got the ball from Jet high on the right wing. Bruce Bowen, the Spurs' best defender, was on you, no surprise. Bowen was five inches shorter than you but would have sliced your Achilles with a machete if he could have figured out how to smuggle one on the court. He was dirtier than a small-town sheriff in a pulp novel. But you didn't give him a chance to use any of his tricks. After a few dribbles, you turned and started to back Bowen down, using your size to get closer to the basket, setting yourself up—everyone assumed—for a turnaround jumper over the smaller player, maybe finding a teammate open around the arc if the Spurs sent a second defender at you.

but

wait

You made a surprise half-spin around Bowen, getting your inside shoulder around him, clearing a path to the rim. Ginobili rose

up with you but wasn't big enough and wasn't in the right position anyway. He stopped you from dunking maybe, but not scoring. He fouled you in the process, sending you to the line to tie the game.

You held a fist pump like you were doing isometrics, your sneer exaggerated by your mouthguard until it was cartoonish, garish, wonderful, and all around you silence, silence never so silent as when 20,000 people are in the presence of it, the genesis of it.

Like any good ending, it had been foreshadowed. You opened the game with a dunk, after shaking Tim Duncan with a fake. In the second quarter, you got around two Spurs for a tough layup and foul, punctuating the play with a celebration that was somewhere between a fist pump and a punch, like you were so overcome you couldn't decide which way to go.

Your free throw was never in doubt.

There were still 21.6 seconds left in regulation. I must have blacked out because I didn't remember that that much time was left until I watched it again recently. We had left Joe out there the entire time, wouldn't let him back into the house out of superstition.

He agreed with the decision.

⊕　⊕　⊕

That 2005–06 season was arguably your best. You averaged a career-high 26.6 points, a figure you'd never top, with 9 rebounds and 2.8 assists. It was your team, finally, after Nash and Finley left, and the Mavs were the best they'd ever been to that point. You were

twenty-seven years old and the best you'd ever been to that point, too.

The 2003 trip to the Western Conference finals might have felt like it arrived a bit too soon. But this was exactly right. It was time and everything had lined up accordingly. The Mavs had swept the Memphis Grizzlies, then led by Pau Gasol, the Spaniard who was your closest competitor for best European player in the league. Game 3 was the only one that was close, and you had saved that one, sending it to overtime with a three-pointer. (I snuck away from a family dinner to see the end.) Then the Spurs had, at long last, been conquered. And, after that, in a perfect narrative twist, the team between you and your first appearance in the Finals was the Suns. Steve.

Going into Game 5, the series was tied. We talked about it a few years later. This is what you told me:

> I've had games where I'm stiff in shootaround, can't make a shot in warmups, and, all of a sudden, you get to the basket one time. You get fouled. You have an and-one. And, all of a sudden, every basket you get, the basket seems to get bigger. I've had experiences where I felt like I could jump out of the gym in the mornings, and I miss my first six, seven shots. The game's weird like that. I've had games where I wasn't feeling well and, for some reason, you can't even get a rebound—somebody seems to tip it, and you end up with zero rebounds. You're seven feet—how the *hell* you not getting one rebound?

And then that night, against Phoenix in the playoffs, it just seems like the ball is coming to you. I was getting offensive rebounds. I was getting good looks at shots. I was driving. I was getting to the foul line. It's just funny how sports works. Sometimes it works in your favor and sometimes it doesn't.

The game before was dreadful for you, just eleven points on three-for-thirteen shooting. In Game 5, you still weren't shooting too well through two quarters and most of another, and to make it worse, you let Suns forward Tim Thomas score twelve points of his own over about three minutes in the third quarter. He taunted you by blowing you a kiss, the Suns up 77–70, you looking at another season "swimming away" as you put it after the game.

No.

Your shot came back. You scored twenty-two points in the fourth alone, the basket getting bigger with each attempt, until the last one—a three with an arc so high it might have been designed by Santiago Calatrava—fell through the net with under two minutes left, splashing in as easily as if you'd launched it at an Olympic pool. Your forty-eighth, forty-ninth, and fiftieth points of the game. You checked out 30 seconds later and the ovation that followed lasted a full minute.

I watched Game 5 at my in-laws' house. I had a superstition in

those days—and I carry traces of it still, a scar that won't ever completely fade—that if the Mavs were doing well, I couldn't change the channel under any circumstances. They could have invited a fifteen-year-old onto the broadcast to roast me with extremely personal and true comments and I would have to remain steadfast. Conversely, if they were on a bad run, I would have to, *have to*, flip to another channel—not for long, just enough to "fix the energy," I told myself—like I was a coach calling a timeout.

My mother-in-law and her husband, my wife's stepfather, came home during the second half. Her stepfather was a bit obsessive about tech, most especially his home theater, where we were watching the game. He came in and wondered why we weren't watching the game in HD—I never could figure out how his setup worked and didn't really care—and then before I could answer or explain my system, he changed the channel. My stomach dropped so hard it felt like I hadn't eaten in weeks.

Despite this, you still somehow got your fifty.

⊕   ⊕   ⊕

After that, Game 6 was a formality. As Adrian Griffin dunked to put the last points on a 102–93 win, finishing the game and the series, you and Steve hugged near the Phoenix basket. If only it had ended then. If *only* it had ended then. If only it had *ended* then. If only it had ended *then*.

If only it had ended then. If only it had ended then. If only it

had ended then. If only it had ended

then. If only it had ended then. If only it had ended then. If only it had ended then. If only it had ended then. If only it had ended then. If only it had ended then. If only it had ended then. If only it had ended then. If only it had ended then. If only it had ended then. If only it had ended then. If only it had ended then. If only it had ended then. If only it had ended then.

If. Only. It. Had. Ended. Then.

You had a rough start to the Finals, scoring just sixteen points,[24] Miami's Udonis Haslem in your uniform like an undershirt. But it was an ugly game for just about everyone on the Mavericks and the Heat, except for Jet Terry, who had thirty-two and four threes. It was sort of a tribute to the mid 1990s, the Heat putting up quarters of thirteen and twelve points. Still, it was a win.

We were there, high up in Section 319. My presence is about all I recall from the game, too high on adrenaline at the beginning and too worn down by the sharp edges at the end.

Game 2 was better. You were back to being the best player on the floor, picking up where you had left off in Phoenix, with twenty-six points and fifteen rebounds, and another win.

I hate to admit this, but the dominant feeling after the first two games of the Finals was boredom. I know I'm not alone. It's not that Mavs fans didn't appreciate being there. I guess it was that it was anticlimactic, after getting past the Spurs and the Suns. Miami, it was like getting into a fistfight in an alley after slaying two dragons. The

---

24. On four for fourteen shooting, missing your first four.

first two games felt like we had rewound to the Grizzlies series: an overmatched team without a compelling back story. This wasn't supposed to be the final boss. No one could focus on the next two games, getting the next two wins, finishing it off. We were past that—some more than others, but everyone at least a little bit. I thought I might not get to go to another game; I had tickets for Game 6. I'm sorry. It felt like the biggest question wasn't if you and the Mavs would win but if the Heat would win any games. After more than a quarter century of trying to get the NBA to take us seriously, we couldn't even savor the moment when we were almost there. I'm so sorry. Anything short of the biggest of wins was not enough.

It goes back a long way.

⊕ ⊕ ⊕

Dallas's inferiority complex was born in the aftermath of the JFK assassination, the sort of outcome you might expect when you suddenly have the nickname "the City of Hate," a reputation bolstered by fact more than opinion, a thread stretching from the 1920s, when Dallas had the biggest chapter of the Ku Klux Klan in the country. Imperial Wizard Hiram W. Evans lived here. One in three eligible men were in the Klan. The state fair held a Klan Day on October 24, 1923, and that night there was the largest initiation ceremony in the cowardly organization's history, with more than six thousand men and women joining. Evans delivered a speech titled "The Menace of Modern Immigration." What a piece of shit.

Forty years after that stain first set, there was the "Mink Coat Mob"—sophisticated, rich, Junior Leaguers, the city's supposed finest families—that accosted Lyndon Johnson and his wife outside a downtown hotel in 1960. General Edwin Walker, a leader of the radical right, a pied piper for the startlingly conservative John Birch Society, had a home off Turtle Creek and it became the HQ of the National Indignation Convention, at one time the country's fastest-growing right-wing organization. And then in November 1963, Dallas, as far as the rest of the country was concerned, killed John F. Kennedy.

Erik Jonsson, son of Swedish immigrants and cofounder of Texas Instruments, was drafted to be mayor of Dallas in the wake, from 1964 to 1971. He was tasked with redeeming the city, setting a new course, creating a new identity from the ashes of what had been. In that way, and on a grander scale, Jonsson was like you—brought in to salvage a disaster.

By the end, Dallas had hustled itself into a new nickname: "The All-American City." Jonnson was behind Goals for Dallas, a program that lasted for twenty years, paying citizens and civic leaders to come up with ambitious plans, big-picture dreams for the city. This is where so much of what Dallas is today comes from, physically and emotionally. Jonnson brought in I.M. Pei to design the pineapple-upside-down-cake City Hall, the tip of a giant arrow that had been shot from a bow in some far-off galaxy and bull's-eyed into a target on the edge of downtown, and he raised money for a new central library across the street, which now bears his name. The recent history of

Dallas is all right there: the starchitect with "world-class" blueprints, the silver-bullet ideas to make everything better immediately. It still happens. It will still happen. Dallas's first impulse is always to cloak insecurity in overwhelming confidence.

In the 1970s, the city had more than its fair share of the latter, but not because of anything it actually did. At the end of the decade, *Dallas* premiered on CBS, and though the goings-on of the show had more in common with a family from Houston,[25] it became our face to the world—scheming strivers wearing ten-gallon Stetsons with suits in mirrored palaces, towers of steel and glass and vanity, rising and falling on the black tide of oil.

The other group that emerged in the 1970s to shape our image was the Dallas Cowboys, essentially another long-running TV show that had little to do with the actual city of Dallas. (The Cowboys left the Cotton Bowl for Texas Stadium in the nearby suburb of Irving in 1971, and never came back.) They were champions, winning two Super Bowls and five conference titles in the decade. But it was Bob Ryan from NFL Films, via the legendary voice of narrator John Facenda, who turned them into *America's Team*, giving rise to Cowboys exceptionalism that still exists decades later and recently with scant evidence to support it.

To me, the city—the modern Dallas—has always had more in

---

25. Its creator, David Jacobs, who had never been to Dallas prior to filming, said as much when he finally came to town, admitting he should have called it *Houston*. Most of the show was filmed in Culver City, California.

common with its basketball team, which began playing a few months after Kristin Shepard shot J.R. Ewing and kicked off a global obsession. We are so worried about being the butt of a joke that we often inevitably become the butt of a joke. No one took us seriously. No one takes us seriously. So we are defensive, but we are proactive about it, which does lead to some good things. We try shit. We take chances. We build parks on tops of highways and draft little-known teenagers from Germany.

But it also creates a restlessness—have you felt it? This permanent search for a one-stop solution, this thirst for acknowledgement. We can be short-sighted, mortgaging the future for the present. And because we want it so much, that recognition, that pat on the head from national or international cognoscenti remains always frustratingly just out of reach. We are a city of dreamers, but sometimes our dreams are both dull and improbable. Who would think that bringing in a brand-name architect would convince outsiders, on its own, that Dallas is a cultural city? But we've done it or tried it at least three times. We are obsessed with appearances when they don't matter so much and relatively uninterested when they actually do, like the condition of streets and the other basic functions of a city. I love Dallas but there are times that I love it like I love a cousin who I pray is not coming to Thanksgiving. I just won't ever agree with how it operates, even as I understand it more. Maybe *because* I understand it more.

That brings us back to 2006.

⊕   ⊕   ⊕

After the first two games of the Finals, we were so excited that an NBA title was near, and with it the external praise that we so crave, that the city lost its mind and somehow allowed the parade route for a Mavericks championship celebration to be published in the *Dallas Morning News*. It was like seeing your own obituary in the paper over your first cup of coffee. They might as well have hurriedly constructed a new arena on top of a Native American burial ground or adopted a herd of black cats while sprinting under a full warehouse inventory of ladders. An unedited crime scene photo would have been less shocking.

Did the team see it?

They must have known how bad it was. I did, but I'm incredibly superstitious, enough that I'm at least OCD-adjacent. We had spit in the face of the basketball gods. You and the rest of the team had been flattened by our hubris, and also maybe Avery Johnson panicked. But, really, I still believe that the city cost the Mavs a championship. Not just with the parade route, but the anxiety running through Dallas like the Trinity after a big rain, more like a lake than a river, an unavoidable presence. Our insecurity was all over, especially as the situation trended toward crisis. We were so desperate to escape being the butt of the joke we became the butt of the joke.

It cost you a bit of your legacy. People say you couldn't have gotten the glory of 2011 without living through the hell of 2006 (and, well, you know) first. But I know you don't believe that. I mean, why *not* both?

You were so close to refuting every argument against you and only ended up strengthening them instead. *Fuck.* Maybe 2006 made you better, made you more determined to win a title. Of course it did. But you didn't need more motivation. You didn't require much improvement. Maybe, sure, you were a better passer later. But you ended 2006 with the second-highest win share total ever at the time, with 5.4.[26] You were always working on your game because you were always working on your game, since you were fifteen, sixteen, with Holger during the offseason and then during the season, too, a couple of weeks at a time. Great players are never truly finished, complete, and they know that and still continue to work to try to get there, and that's what makes them great. More than the erosion of skills or production, that's what causes them to eventually stop. The effort it takes to become great and the effort it takes to not only maintain that level but build upon it, expand it, conquer more and more and more, is mentally and physically exhausting. You are walking uphill with a knapsack full of stones, and you just keep adding more to it the higher you go, the longer you walk. First there are elements to be added or honed, a new shot or a bit of footwork. Then fitness, more and heavier weights, yoga, stretching, running on the beach to strengthen knees and ankles, naps in a hyperbaric chamber to get more oxygen in your lungs. Then as you get older, it's your diet. No more beer. No more sugar. Everything for fuel, nothing for fun.

---

26. LeBron James would get to 5.8 in 2012. At the time, only Tim Duncan's 5.9 in 2003 was better.

To do it for a long time, at a high level, as you know better than anyone, means it becomes one long never-ending season, no breaks, just a pause for a new schedule to be loaded into the system.

⊕ ⊕ ⊕

For most of Game 3, up until halfway through the fourth quarter, it did appear that you guys were most likely on your way to a sweep. I was watching at home and stupidly thinking stupid thoughts like, *I'm surprised this isn't harder*, and it's amazing how quickly you can become entitled. I'm assuming it's something like getting very rich very quickly and forgetting you ever weren't, that you started out by selling books out of a garage, but I've thus far never become even kind of rich really slowly, so it's a guess. You would know, but you've never seemed to care about money, so maybe both of us would just be guessing.

It's also amazing, and unfortunate, how quickly comeuppance can arrive.

This was reversal of fortune with the turning radius of a smart car. Figure skaters spin slower. The Mavs took a lead with five minutes left in the third quarter; with 6:34 left in the fourth, it had been built up to thirteen points. The fact that Dwyane Wade had checked back in seemed almost irrelevant. What was he going to do?

We were all suddenly aboard a 747 made of wax, flying higher and higher, aiming for the sun.

Wade hit a fourteen-footer over you, as you backpedaled trying to stop him. Then he got a layup with a foul, drawn on Josh Howard. Then a seventeen-foot jumper after a three by James Posey. Then

another layup. Then, following a pair of free throws by Shaq, a twenty-footer from the baseline, and Miami was down only one point with 1:16 left, and Jimmy Buffett and all the Heat fans were losing their minds, and watching a double-digit lead leak away in front of a crazed Jimmy Buffett seems like it would just make the entire experience worse.

I don't want to keep going, but we have to.

And no matter what I know is coming in a few years from this point, it's still nauseating to think about, let alone watch. I don't. I haven't. Miami took the lead on free throws by Haslem and Posey, Devin Harris tied it with a layup, and a ring-chasing Gary Payton swung it back to Miami with a long two to beat the shot clock, his only field goal of the game. There were nine seconds left.

Do you still think about what happened next?

You got the ball and drove to the hoop on Haslem, picking up the foul. You were nine of ten from the line at that point. Mike Breen underlined that on the ABC broadcast: "Again, one of the best free-throw shooters in the NBA: 90 percent during the playoffs, 90 percent during the regular season."

You made the first, giving you thirty points for the game. The second . . .

rimmed . . .

out.

You fouled Wade after the rebound.

The game was over.

It was my thirty-second birthday.

The game was over and so was the series; the cancer was already killing it but hadn't shown up on the scans yet.

After that gut punch of a loss, it wasn't a surprise that Game 4 was a blowout Miami win. The overtime loss in Game 5 is the one that still rankles all these years later. Wade was twenty-one of twenty-five on foul shots—exactly the same as the entire Mavs team. But, to be fair, he was also making tough shots and taking it right at you guys.

You'd almost gotten the win in regulation, hitting a frankly ridiculous, spinning, leaning jumper at the free-throw line, then finding Erick Dampier inside for a dunk, passing off the dribble and over the defense, "Birdesque" a correct comparison for once. And in overtime, you got a chance at redemption for Game 3. It was almost the same scenario, down by one with under thirty seconds left. This time, you hit a nineteen-foot jumper after dribbling to your right, almost losing it, then fading away over Shaq, the kind of shot I used to take on my hoop in the driveway.

Nine seconds were left.

It should have held up.

Wade got the ball, of course, dribbled around you and two other Mavs, and threw up a wild shot. This I have watched. Dozens of times. Hundreds, maybe. I still don't see the foul referee B-----t S-------e called on you. I still don't understand. In real time, I was Derek Harper in 1984, thinking the Mavs had won. I was watching at Eric's house again, where we had locked Joe outside at the end of the Spurs game. It was a couple of blocks away from home. I left immediately

after Wade's winning free throws and walked into the dark. Across the street, one of Eric's neighbors screamed into the lightless night and threw an unidentified object against his wooden fence.

⊕ ⊕ ⊕

I don't remember much about Game 6, even though I was there. I do remember the end, the last few seconds. I remember Jet missing a three that would have tied it and the Heat getting the rebound and then Antoine Walker celebrating down below us, high-kneeing along the baseline, and that made it worse. I didn't hate Walker, don't hate Walker, but he wasn't good in Dallas and, in my mind, is forever wearing that Hefty bag uniform.

I remember wanting to be out of the building, *needing* to be out the building. But the people at the end of our row, a father and son, wouldn't get up. The father ran a pest control company that had a memorably bad local TV commercial that featured the kid he brought to games, and I guess it did well enough to afford him tickets in our section (so: not that well) and a jersey that he wore to the games with no shirt underneath it. You have to be five years old or in insane shape to pull that off, and he was neither, I'm sorry.

They just sat there dumbly, and I get it, *I got it*, but I couldn't abide it just then. I pushed past them brusquely, and I wanted to apologize right away but I didn't, just kept going, down the stairs, into the night, then into the train, and as soon as I boarded taking the train felt like the stupidest thing I could have done, and probably was. It was dead quiet, uncomfortable, the type of absence of sound that is

almost deafening. And then into that void came the man in the seat behind us, who started loudly, and I'm assuming drunkenly, talking about how you had blown it, and my fists clenched and unclenched over and over until they ached. No one wanted him to keep talking but no one wanted to engage him either, to open the door to the frustration banging on it. That argument would have turned into a fight and that fight would not have ended well for anyone involved and I knew it and I think everyone in that train car knew it, too, and maybe even that's what he wanted. To feel something else, anything else. I don't know.

He kept going until I guess even he couldn't take it anymore. I don't remember anything after that.

⊕   ⊕   ⊕

I flew to Chicago a couple of years later to interview Wade for a cover story for the magazine a satellite cable company put out. Basically, a glorified channel guide. It paid well.

I wanted to hate Wade and I told him so not long into the conversation. But he was perfectly nice, and answered all my questions thoughtfully and seemingly truthfully, just as you have always done. I was thankful and disappointed at the same time. I suppose I wanted him to be a villain, or to remain one.

While Wade was getting his portrait taken, in various poses and outfits, his son Zaire found a basketball and badgered me until I agreed to guard him. He crossed me over almost immediately and I felt like the Heat had beaten the Mavs all over again.

7

Sometimes Style Can Get You Killed

I didn't lose the mayoral election like the 2006 Mavs. I lost it like the 2007 Mavs. As in: after some surprising success, I wasn't even there at the end.

I wasn't very good or pretty good or, let's say, even adequate at traditional political skills, like public speaking or fundraising. I got better at the former over time and somehow even worse at the latter. But I was able to leverage what I did know—writing, music, Being Extremely Online—into something resembling a viable candidacy. *Esquire* asked me to write about my campaign (headline: "The MySpace Candidate," lol). We had learned from a source with another candidate that we were polling third (in a crowded twelve-person field) in name recognition among potential voters. And with the traditionally low turnout numbers, it wouldn't take much.

In March, less than two months before the election, we borrowed a convertible VW Beetle and put the rest of our cash into ZC/07 T-shirts and beads, and I rode in the Greenville Avenue St. Patrick's Day Parade. I had been in Austin the night before for the SXSW music festival, since I still had a day job mostly writing about

pop culture for a magazine. I left around four in the morning, without having gone to bed at all, to make it back in time for the parade. (I took a nap at a rest stop for an hour.) Most of our previous campaign events had been on our home court, in front of audiences we mostly knew or were reliably friendly. We had no idea what would happen when we went public. It ended up being the best day, easily, of the entire run.

I remember at one point, not far from the route's end, the parade stopped. People on both sides of the street screamed out my name and various encouraging phrases as I tossed shirts and beads until I ran out, and they kept cheering for me, and it would have been the part of the movie where the music swelled, and in my head and heart it did, and it felt like, not like I *would* win, but that I *could* win, or at least that was the first time I allowed myself to consider the possibility, to open myself up entirely to it no matter the cost. When was the first time you felt that? 2003? 2006? I felt it then and I felt it later when I fell in love again and allowed myself to look at the future, not just next week or next month but ten years down the road, twenty, and it's terrifying a little, but also exhilarating, your body lit up like a lantern from inside, your head fucking pounding from smiling. That's how it felt in March 2007, too. That Saturday.

A week later, I was out of the race.

It was a Monday afternoon, and I was working from home. The city secretary called to tell me that my petition to get on the ballot had been rejected. A potential candidate had to get, if I'm remembering correctly, one half of one percent of the total votes cast in the previous mayoral election to sign your petition. Since Dallas had, and

has, a pitiful voting record, it was only around seven hundred signatures. And we'd fallen short by thirty or so, even though we had collected almost a thousand—more than enough, we had thought.

Here's what happened. My first campaign manager left in January (he'd say he was fired; I'd say he quit; it was probably in the middle) and my new one couldn't start for a few weeks. My lawyer, who had been keeping an eye on when to start gathering signatures, was distracted, happily, with the birth of his second child. I was finishing writing a book, working full-time, and trying to keep up with the other candidates, as well as my wife and not-quite-three-year-old son. When we finally figured out it was past time to circulate the petition, we had less than a week or so. We had to improvise. The community college interns we brought on to help went to the one place we told them to avoid (the parking lot of a Walmart on the edge of town). A lot of the names they collected ended up being ineligible to vote in a Dallas city election; they were county voters. That is an explanation, but not an excuse. We fucked up. *I* fucked up. And it was deeply embarrassing.

You know better than anyone else in Dallas, or anywhere else, what it's like to have one of your best days and one of your worst separated by only a week or two. And it happened the same year. 2007 was a real motherfucker, huh?

⊕   ⊕   ⊕

Can we maybe agree that the 2006–07 season was a long con, a "Big Store" scam that the rest of the NBA was in on, an elaborate plot

that involved twenty-nine teams and thousands of other confeder-
ates? Let's say that "Rookie of the Year Brandon Roy" was played
by a Julliard-trained actor named Andrew Cleft, and he got so into
character that he ended up playing five more seasons in the league
before returning to the theater company he founded. We can see now,
in hindsight, how it almost fell apart a few times, as some of the narrative flourishes strained the credulity of the marks (a.k.a. you and
me and everyone in Dallas). I mean, come on: one team with separate winning streaks of twelve, thirteen, eight, and seventeen games?
Winning sixty-seven games after losing the first four? Doing all that
after collapsing in the Finals the previous season? It was almost too
much.

But that's why these audacious confidence schemes work.
People *want* to believe the impossible is possible, that it *can* happen to them, that money falls from the sky, that a team can bounce
back from a disastrous, demoralizing, soul-crushing failure on the
sport's biggest stage and deliver not only the best regular season
in franchise history, but one of the best in the entire history of the
league—sixty-seven wins, and it wasn't seventy only because your
coach pulled up short of the finish line and decided to jog across,
resting key players over the last few weeks, when you guys picked
up four of your fifteen losses in just eighteen days. People wanted
to believe in you, their leader, the face of the franchise, the man who
had taken the loss to Miami the hardest, who would have been forgiven if he had decided he'd had enough and went back to Europe
to finish his career, who would have been understood if he had come

back a bit shell-shocked, if he had maybe not been all-in anymore, if he retreated to protect himself. But you didn't. You gave them every reason to believe, coming back stronger than ever, joining the NBA's 50-40-90 club[27] while delivering your best season, the league's best season, and finally winning the MVP trophy.

People, sports fans in particular, want to believe that something like this can happen, and that is why they are so easy to set up, why they never see the endgame coming. They won't realize it was all a lie, a way to wrest from them their last shred of pride. A Big Score requires a big lie, and 2006–07 was the biggest. Having your first coach, your American father, be the one to finish off the con was maybe an unnecessary touch, a mean twist, but it made a sort of poetic sense, and I have to appreciate it on that level.

_____

27. That's shooting 50 percent from the field, 40 percent from three, and 90 percent from the free-throw line. Until then, it had only been done by Larry Bird, Steve Nash, Reggie Miller, and Mark Price; Kevin Durant, Steph Curry, and Malcolm Brogdon have done it since.

If only.

That it happened on its own was crueler. Winning nearly seventy games just to get embarrassed in the biggest way possible *and* having Nellie be behind it all. That it happened to you, in that way, after everything else, was the cruelest of all. Like I said, very few people have their best and worst moments within a week or two of each other. The ones who do usually have done something to deserve it. I'm sure I brought that hell on myself.

But not you. You didn't deserve 2007. The fact that you played eleven seasons after that one feels like a miracle sometimes. Eleven games might have been more than some could manage. I never would have come back from Australia, where you disappeared for several weeks after the season. Suffering my own minor-key failure a few months earlier, and unable to actually vanish, I instead disappeared from myself. I didn't cut my hair or beard for a year after bombing out of the mayoral race.

⊕ ⊕ ⊕

2007.

I knew that you were in trouble, that we were in trouble, as soon as the lineups were announced for the first game in the Mavs' first-round series against the Golden State Warriors. Instead of the usual starting five that had dominated the rest of the league, on the way to sixty-seven wins, Avery Johnson had replaced center Erick Dampier[28]

---

28. I wouldn't say I was exactly looking forward to Erick Dampier—whom I

with small forward Devean George. It was clear insecurity had taken over. The team was trying to be something it was not.

You guys had lost all three regular-season games against the Warriors, but one was at the beginning, before the team really got rolling, and one was at the end, when the team was coasting along, just trying to avoid injuries. An 0–3 record wasn't necessarily representative. Changing to match up with a No. 8 seed that had just snuck into the playoffs gave the Warriors—now known forever as the "We Believe!" Warriors—a confidence boost. And, as you always say, the NBA is a confidence league. So it wasn't a white flag, but it absolutely was a red one. Everyone knew from that moment that Johnson was scared of his former boss.

But replacing Dampier with George was more or less Avery's only tactical decision. When it came time to really respond, when the situation took on an unforeseen desperation, when it was time to come up with a way to free you from Golden State's defensive strategy, he did nothing. He turned you into a basketball Robinson Crusoe, stranding you on Pinch Post Island.

It was obvious from the beginning that Nellie had a plan for you, his former protégé. He knew you as well as almost anyone,

---

referred to as "Pan Hands," who once took two colleagues out for sushi and made them pay—play center. But he'd been doing it all season, and that had worked, so I wasn't hoping to see a change during the first game of the playoffs and I certainly didn't expect it to happen. Avery was the one who wanted Dampier on the team in the first place! They had been teammates at Golden State and he advocated for acquiring him in the summer of 2005.

and so he was familiar with your strengths and weaknesses, the tiny cracks that could become a chasm. *Of course* he knew what to do with you. It was like when it was revealed that Batman had compiled files on exactly how to defeat the other members of the Justice League. Nellie defended you with a smaller player—which wouldn't work on its own for a full game, not to mention an entire series, so he had another player attack you from the blind side. It wasn't about forcing you into bad shots or smartly defending good ones. The idea was to not let you shoot at all. That tactic turned into a triple team, with your own frustration becoming a third defender. The Warriors didn't have anyone with your combination of size and quickness, but they did have natural irritants like Matt Barnes (who got a tattoo the size of a dessert plate on his neck during the series) and Stephen Jackson, the kind of tough players who seemed like they were playing in jeans and Timberlands.

Could all of that have been overcome by having you catch the ball on the move or further away from the basket or any spot where you weren't so susceptible to another defender coming from over your shoulder, behind your back, where you couldn't see? If Avery had let you play like you always had before, shooting threes whenever you wanted, playing without a governor? Perhaps. But no one will ever know, because Avery kept you in your familiar spots, kept the offense the same, stuck to his guns even though both barrels were glued to his feet. You didn't lose to the Warriors and Nelson on your own. Avery just made it look that way.

It was like you had two coaches working against you.

⊕ ⊕ ⊕

The sixth and final game was especially brutal. You missed your first nine shots, finally getting one to fall with 38.7 seconds left in the first half. It tied the score at forty-six. Then, seven seconds later, Baron Davis hit a three and that was it. You didn't make another basket until the fourth quarter, and that was the only other one you made. By then the game and the series and the season were all but over.

On the way back to the locker room after the twenty-five-point loss, after the Mavs became the first No. 1 seed to fall to a No. 8 since the first round was expanded to seven games—and just the third ever—you picked up a trash can and threw it, gouging a hole in a wall twelve feet up.

Were you even aware you did it?

The Warriors never repaired the hole. It was a battle scar, a reminder of what they accomplished, long before the revolution and the titles and the dynasty. Instead, they covered it with a piece of Plexiglas and hung a bright yellow "We Believe!" T-shirt above it. And around 2012, after you had gotten your ring, you autographed the Plexiglas.[29]

"Until then, I was still mad about it," you told ESPN's Tim MacMahon in 2014. "Oh, I'm still mad about it. We had a great shot that year, we won sixty-seven games, and, to me, it was another lost

---

29. The Warriors cut out the shrine after their final home game at Oracle in 2019 and moved it across the bay to their new home in San Francisco.

opportunity. I think we played the Spurs really, really well that year. I think we beat them a couple of times and we figured that if we see them, we might have a chance of going all the way. The Spurs ended up sweeping the Cavs that year. That's another year I look back at as a lost opportunity, but it's part of my past and it made me a better player."

It did, you're right, lead you to develop the shot that will forever be associated with you, the leg-up, leaned-back fadeaway, the silhouette that instantly comes to mind when your name is mentioned. It is iconic. The series would eventually recede from view as the defining moment of your career, becoming part of the story instead of the conclusion. But that was all a few years away. At the time, after knocking that hole in the wall, I know you wanted to crawl inside of it and disappear. The best stretch of your career was now bracketed by its two lowest moments, another disappointment, another almost, another another another. You wanted to go somewhere, anywhere.

except

You knew you couldn't leave. Not yet. You didn't *know* know, but you were pretty sure. You asked the team and the team asked the league and the league said to stay put.

In a couple of weeks, you would be named the NBA's MVP, the first European player to win the award. Normally, at that time, the winner would receive the award during the second round of the playoffs, prior to one of the home games. But since the Mavs were out of home games for a few months, it meant some other ceremony, a press

conference probably, having to be in front of people when that was the absolute last thing you wanted. You found out for sure just a few days before it happened.

"Everything was so fresh," you told me later. "I felt embarrassed, I think, more than anything. We won [almost] seventy games and, all of a sudden, we're a first-round exit. First couple of days, I just thought: *Don't give it to me.*"

You couldn't run away, but you could try to hide in a bottle, twelve days sliding by in a blurry smear, most of it in your Highland Park home, the old one, your bachelor pad. That's where you found out. Your friend Brian Dameris told me about it.

"We were just kind of lying around, hungover after one of our bender nights trying to get through the sorrow of what had happened, and he was looking at his phone, and he got a text and he just kind of, while staring at the ceiling, he said, 'I got it.' And I'm like, 'What? You got what?' And he says, 'I got the MVP.' I jumped up and was like, 'Oh my gosh!' as I kind of realized what was happening, and he was just sheepish about it.

"Eventually, we celebrated and had a great time, but I think his initial reaction was he didn't deserve it because he let the city and the team down because they lost in the playoffs. It really struck me that nothing could've been further from the truth. He'd just gotten the biggest honor the league could bestow and he was upset that they'd lost and that he'd let the city down. I think people saw that and saw who he was and was doing everything he could for the city and wasn't a prima donna."

It's not a sentiment you hear from Dallas athletes very often, maybe because the Cowboys are ours in name only and the Rangers have always belonged to the suburbs. Athletes in general, these days, aren't in the same place long enough to bond with a city the way you did.

But anyway, you hadn't let us down. You'd only shown you were one of us.

⊕   ⊕   ⊕

A couple of years later, someone in the Mavs organization told me how they saw it.

"Dirk is the focal point of us turning this franchise around, and he put this thing on his freaking back and took us to the Finals, and then, alright, after the Finals—there were lots of things, adjustments that weren't made, and who took the brunt of that whole thing? And if you remember the press conference, it was lots of folks that didn't mind side-stepping a little heat and it all fell on him. *Oh, Dirk can't do it. You talk about a meltdown. He's weak. He's European.* He's all these things, and the disappointment, to me, was that was kind of allowed to happen. And he stood up to those cameras and he took it and he didn't bitch and moan and complain. He took it.

"And then the next year was the Golden State meltdown, and guess what? It was the same frickin' song and dance, you know? It was, *Oh, well, Dirk couldn't do this and couldn't make the big shot.* Now, some of that goes with being the best player on the team. But

Dirk is a player that needs, in order for you to fully utilize what he can or can't do, you can't put him in a box. You can't force Dirk to be some center that's gonna take ten dribbles à la Charles Barkley, back you down in the middle of the paint, and dunk on you. You gotta give him the freedom to do things and make his three-point shot, and so, basically, Dirk was fighting with one arm tied behind his back.

"And did he bitch? Did he say, 'Hey, I wish I could shoot a three on occasion'? Did he bleed to the press or some secret ghost-writer? 'Man, if I had been under a more creative coach or this or that'—you never heard one of those things from him. Dirk doesn't do that. He takes it, internalizes it. Whether we win a championship here or not"—and that was still up in the air—"the fact that Dirk has shouldered this blame, responsibility, however you want to quantify it, from the national media—he's not this enough or that enough—to me is a bunch of bullshit."

Someone should read this at your Hall of Fame induction.

⊕   ⊕   ⊕

Almost two weeks after the Mavs were knocked out of the playoffs, you accepted your MVP trophy.

You showed up in a dark pinstripe suit, so far away from the kid meeting reporters in a room like that wearing the first suit he'd ever owned, and you smiled and you posed with Commissioner David Stern and the trophy and Cuban and Avery. You faced up to it, got through it, answered the questions as best you could. (Better than

Cuban, who choked up talking about you: "He's not the guy you wonder if he cares, he's the guy who hurts so much when things don't go the way he wants.")

Yes, it's a great honor. Yes, I'm disappointed. Yes, I want to win a title. Yes, it's good to see that Europeans can play basketball, too. No, I don't know what the team needs.

"For me, at this stage right now," you said, "I feel like it's a little hard for me to be happy because of the way the season ended with the postseason. This is an award for the regular season and that's the way I've got to look at it, and I'm extremely proud. It means that you play on a high level for a lot of months, a lot of games. The last ten days, a lot of things go through your mind after the season ended. And we can be proud of what we did in this regular season. Sixty-seven wins is a very, very special season and there are few teams that have won more games that have won more than we did. I try to look at it in that way and try to be positive and just enjoy this day for me. This award is not only for me; I never really liked personal awards. I've always been about the team. This is a team sport and so I want to thank this whole franchise that drafted me and gave me a chance to be a franchise player."

You left for Germany, for home, the next day, and had a press conference there, too. And then you disappeared into Australia for five weeks. As far as I was concerned, the 2007 season disappeared with you. I didn't watch another game.

⊕   ⊕   ⊕

You went to Australia with your old friend and coach Holger Geschwindner, of course—time for another lesson. He had never really stopped teaching you, coming to Dallas a couple times a year to tune up your game. The Mavs set him up with an office at their Deep Ellum facility.

You flew to Sydney first and went to the famous Jørn Utzon-designed Opera House, like a stack of conquistador helmets floating on the water, catching a performance of Beethoven's Fourth and Seventh Symphonies. Then: into the wild. You set out into the Outback, across the Central Plains toward Uluru, a hunk of sandstone also known as Ayers Rock that juts one thousand feet into the air and three miles below the surface, and surely that was a metaphor for something. You and Holger had rented a four-wheel-drive Jeep with a removable roof and two beds. You were unofficially on what Australians call "temporary mobility" now, an Aboriginal rite of passage, and it was the right time. You were entering a new life cycle, shedding the previous one, making the transition into the rest of your career. The rest of your life. The things you craved—a championship, a family—they were all so close. But you didn't know that.

You and Holger camped out, sleeping in the Jeep, sitting around campfires, drinking whiskey from the bottle, not shaving, rarely bathing. You were Desmond Hume in *Lost*, drunk and bearded, wondering why fate had forsaken you.

After Uluru, it was on to the Olgas, a huddle of bornhardts—large, domed, red-orange rocks, another sacred place to Australia's Aboriginal people. In fact, you and Holger were on one of their

ancient paths, followed for thousands of years. The destination: spiritual rebirth. Did you know this?

Maybe that wasn't the point of the trip, maybe it was really just getting away from everything as far as you possibly could, but that's what you needed, a hard reboot, a return to what basketball meant to you, what was important in your life, where you were at two years before all of this; ten years ago, before the league; twenty years from then, when it wouldn't matter anymore. You and Holger traveled from the Great Dividing Range to the Western Plateau, across the dry plains in the Central Basin. You vanished, in a way, with no real connection to time or the outside world. You hiked up mountains and down canyons, just as you had done together years ago, when Holger took you to the Grand Canyon on that American college trip just to see how you would hold up. You went back to Sydney, then the Great Barrier Reef, snorkeling and napping on the beach; to New Zealand and Tahiti and Northern Australia, a few days at a time, never thinking further ahead than that in the present, but talking about the future always, not really the next season but the next decade, the next chapter of your life.

By the time the trip was over, you had shaken off the loss to the Warriors. You were still sad but no longer consumed. Golden State had won more than you and the Mavs had lost.

"It seemed like every game they would hit a crazy shot," you said in November, once you were back in Dallas. "Like, Baron Davis would hit a leaner from half court or something, bank it off the glass. They were on fire."

You were just twenty-nine years old, but people had already

written you off, at least as the kind of superstar who can lead a team to a championship. For the next couple of years, it looked as though that might be true.

But you were just getting ready.

⊕ ⊕ ⊕

On June 14, the San Antonio Spurs finished off a four-game sweep of LeBron James and the Cavaliers in Cleveland. French point guard Tony Parker was named MVP. Michael Finley, your old friend, finally won a championship, and went home with the game ball. I could only wonder what might have been.

Two days later, Tom Leppert, the CEO of a construction company, defeated three-term city councilman Ed Oakley—with only 49,558 votes—to become mayor of Dallas. Leppert and Oakley had made it into the runoff election with 19,367 and 14,754 votes, respectively.

Again, I could only wonder what might have been.

Leppert didn't do much for the city during his short stint as mayor; he left before his first term was complete to pursue a run for the United States Senate, a doomed enterprise that saw him fail to make it out of the Republican primary, coming in a distant third. All we have to show for Leppert's time in office is a convention center hotel in downtown that we didn't really need and that he refused to let the developer pay for, insisting that the city would foot the bill. We're still paying.

2007 really was a motherfucker.

8

We Didn't Know the Future, but We Did What Was Right

Here is something I completely forgot about: *Sports Illustrated* picked you and the Mavericks to win the championship in 2008. "No more setbacks for this favorite, which will finally be the last one standing." There are no howlers in the write-up that accompanies it, though in retrospect it makes it clear that Avery Johnson's main plan (maybe only plan) was, "Dirk, do more, *please*." According to writer Gene Menez, in the offseason Avery told you that you needed "to become a better passer, offensive rebounder, and defender," and also that he asked you "to take on more of a leadership role," and, OK, did he want you to lay out the uniforms before games and entertain at halftime, too? Avery was as spoiled as we all were, so used to your greatness that we took it for granted, assumed it was an endlessly renewable resource, and that it could be refined further, expanded to cover more areas, hide more flaws, that no one else need do anything because you had it handled, and that's just unfair. None of us have always deserved you.

The Mavs, of course, were not the last ones standing at the end of 2008, everyone knows, but if you recall, it wasn't even close. The

154

team won sixteen fewer games, barely made the playoffs, and were knocked out pretty quickly and easily by a New Orleans Hornets team featuring point guard Chris Paul and your future teammates Tyson Chandler and Peja Stojaković. I watched part of the first game during a break in the Passover Seder at my wife's aunt's in-laws' house and knew the season was really over, and it felt like everything was over, like I was watching the future and the Mavs weren't in it any longer.

Change happens fast in the NBA.

⊕   ⊕   ⊕

Like 2003–04, the 2007–08 season was a comedown and largely forgettable—and it provided me with one personal highlight. I've asked you about it a couple of times, but we end up talking about something else before I get a real answer.

It happened during Jason Kidd's seventh game with the Mavericks—or, rather, his second seventh game, after the Hall of Fame point guard was traded back to the team, in exchange for Devin Harris. Kidd and you and his new-old team were squaring off against Kobe Bryant and the Lakers on ABC's Sunday-afternoon NBA showcase. It was the Mavs' coming-out party after a trade that was necessary for the franchise and for you, both still a little adrift after 2006 and 2007. Kidd's homecoming came during a stretch when even diehard Mavs fans had at least slightly stopped paying attention. Other than the *SI* season preview, the team had been removed from the

group of serious title contenders, even though nothing had changed. Which I guess was the point. The Mavs had won sixty-seven games with these players. But they had also lost to the Heat and, worse, the Warriors with these players. There was a haunted aspect to the team and bringing in journeyman wing Trenton Hassell was probably not a big enough smudge stick to change the energy. There had to be more. Trading for Kidd was the first move.

"We needed a change," you told me a year later. "I felt great with him. I had fun again, I was running, I got open looks again. What he's so great at, he sees stuff developing. With other point guards, you'd get the ball once you were open, and once you get it, they'd already closed out. Well, he already sees that, hey, this guy might be open, so the pass is already on the way—when you might not be open *yet*. But it comes to you right when you're open for that split second. And Steve was kind of the same way, so I'm lucky in my career to play with two Hall of Fame point guards."

But it was clear that was not the only transaction necessary. Firing Johnson and replacing him with Rick Carlisle would follow after the season.

You were, personally, in the trough between the crests of two waves. Losing to the Warriors, losing to the man who'd helped build you, that ended your first prime, and it would take another season before the second started. You needed time to synthesize what you had learned from Nelson and Johnson and combine that with Carlisle's new system and the freedom it afforded you. Your friend Brian Dameris put it to me like this: "I think Rick brought the best of

what Nellie did and what Avery did together to make him the well-rounded player that he is, and on a personal level, I think as he got confidence because he was playing better, he got more swagger in the locker room."

You also needed time for the organization to put together a roster that was ready for you to lead, mostly by example, with the resolve that you found in the Australian wilderness and the shot you developed that no one would be able to easily defend. That would come. But not in 2008.

It's strange to look back and see just how much of an afterthought you were then. Your numbers were not far off those of your MVP campaign the year before—and you didn't even make the top ten in MVP voting.[30] You were entirely out of the conversation.

The only reason the Mavs were being talked about on that Sunday afternoon, March 2, was because of the Kidd trade. The thirty-four-year-old guard held up his end that day, finishing with fifteen points (including three three-pointers), eleven assists, six rebounds, and four steals. Unsurprisingly, though, the game turned into a duel between you and Kobe. He had fifty-two points, with twenty-two in the fourth quarter and another eight in overtime. You had thirty and the three-pointer that brought about the bonus period (where the Mavs would fall, 108–104).

Despite all of that, it is a mostly forgotten contest to everyone

---

30. Your stats: 23.6 points, 8.6 rebounds, 3.5 assists on 48/36/88 shooting percentages. You finished eleventh, after Manu Ginobili.

aside from me and my friend Bob, who is a Lakers fan. I once took him to a Mavs-Lakers game in Dallas and he started an M-V-P! chant for Kobe. It's safe to say that he feels the same about him that I feel about you.

I had watched most of the game from my couch. Then I had to drive to Arlington, about half an hour away, so I listened to the fourth quarter on the radio and overtime sitting in a parking lot. Because of that, I didn't notice what had happened. But Bob did and he immediately texted to tell me. He later sent a clip of the exchange that I have somewhere on a phone three or four phones ago.

What was on it, was this: Kobe is at the free-throw line and looks over at you, doing that hooded-eyed, chin-jutting, cocky smile, a gesture that began as a faithful impression of Michael Jordan but became its own thing over the years, more of a caricature, more belonging to him. And then he said it:

I
SEE YOU,
BIG GERMAN.

I
SEE YOU.

I see you, Big German.

It became sort of a mantra. Big shot—*I see you, Big German.* Good play—*I see you, Big German.* Funny tweet—*I see you, Big German.* For the next decade, sometimes at Mavs games, sometimes when I was just watching on TV or my phone, it was my personal "I am Groot," the only thing I could say and the only thing I wanted to.

I see you, Big German.

Had anyone from L.A. ever acknowledged that Dallas mattered in any way? You didn't need the external validation, but the organization did. The city did. And it was perfect that it came from Kobe. Casey Smith, the Mavs head trainer since 2004, worked with Bryant with the U.S. Men's National Team. He told me in 2009 that "from an overall standpoint of how Dirk approaches things, how he takes care of his body, his nutrition—the guy that most closely resembles him that I've ever worked with is Kobe."

I really thought the two of you would be tied together, in some way, forever. That you would have more time with each other once you were both retired. We'd see you joking around together before Mavs games in Los Angeles, or maybe Kobe's interests would bring him to Dallas for a film festival or a girls' basketball tournament and we'd spot you chatting just off the court at the AAC. You'd be there at each other's Hall of Fame induction ceremonies. Maybe he would say it then, too, spotting you out in the crowd, another guy who knew what it took to be great, the sacrifices, what you'd give up and what you'd gain. He'd point and say, "I see you, Big German."

But it was not to be.

Kobe and his thirteen-year-old daughter, Gigi, along with seven others, were killed in a helicopter crash on January 26, 2020, on the way to a basketball game. "It's so sad," you said a few days later. "It's something I don't think I'll ever get over."

⊕ ⊕ ⊕

There was one more low moment before it all started to point up again.

From the beginning, you always responded to every question asked of you truthfully and thoughtfully, not hiding behind clichés or simply avoiding an answer altogether. If you were scared, you said so. If you were struggling, you admitted as much. Pride or masculinity or gamesmanship precludes honesty in many athletes, maybe most of them, and their coaches, too, and, frankly, most men.

Never you. Before you joined the Mavericks, you said you weren't sure if you were ready, and it wasn't a bargaining ploy, to guarantee more playing time or to go to the team of your choosing. You were simply openly talking about your feelings. It's difficult for people to handle that level of honesty, and so they make fun of it, consider it a character flaw. They run from it, as if they might get infected. Especially when it comes to sports. We expect you guys to be warriors and then attack when you are at your most brave. It's a flaw in *our* character.

But you never changed. Sometimes you are so straightforward that people hear something that isn't there, that doesn't exist. Which

brings us to the 2009 playoffs, the second-round series against the Denver Nuggets.

You were talking about how the Nuggets were defending you, remember? You said: "I think Birdman [Chris Andersen] does a good job because he's so long. He contests my shot. [Kenyon] Martin and Nenê are stronger, and they try to body me more, and Birdman's just long, and when I shoot he can still jump up there and contest the shot. So, yeah, they've got three very good defenders."

The hosts of TNT's *Inside the NBA* took what amounted to a recitation of a scouting report as an admission of weakness, a lack of confidence, proof that you weren't a leader. That you *couldn't* be a leader.

Chris Webber: "I've never heard a scorer, I've never heard a true warrior, say, *This guy can check me*."

Kenny Smith: "It feeds the stereotype that this guy is playing a little soft."

Charles Barkley: "That pisses me off every time I hear that. If a guy even thought he could guard me, I'd tell him, 'I'm going to kick your ass tonight.'"

The Mavs lost that series, but it wasn't because any of the Nuggets could guard you or that you thought any of them could. Even with an in-his-prime Carmelo Anthony on the other side, you were the high scorer on both teams in every game, averaging 34.4 points for the series. You also led both teams in rebounding. And you did all that while dealing with an actual real-life problem and not some controversy ginned up by three former players and "three very good defenders."

Between Games 2 and 3, your ex-fiancée Cristal Taylor was arrested at your home on two outstanding warrants.[31] You had discovered her past after hiring a private investigator, on the advice of Holger and others, to do a background check in advance of a prenup agreement and broke off the engagement. While in jail, Taylor claimed that she was pregnant. One local reporter caused a scene at a press conference, getting angry at you for supposedly abandoning your unborn child behind bars, and then went on a popular morning radio show to double down on his accusation. (It was later revealed that Taylor wasn't pregnant, with your child or anyone else's, and the reporter eventually quit his job to launch a wildly unsuccessful bid for Congress.)

And yet: *This guy is playing a little soft.* Soft! It would be hard to deny that at least some of their criticism was drawn from long-held ideas about European players, for the most part white ones, a stereotype that Smith alluded to.

You were in the middle of one of your best playoff series, succeeding despite facing three very good defenders, all while the off-court future you thought you were building was imploding dramatically and publicly. You were such a private person that no one even really knew you had a girlfriend, much less a fiancée. Your life, what people could see of it, was mostly on the court. It wasn't like

---

31. A probation violation stemming from a conviction in Missouri and a theft of services charge that she had been indicted on in Beaumont, Texas, in 2006; Taylor allegedly didn't pay a dentist for work worth between $1,500 and $20,000.

the early days, when you and Steve were hanging out at The Loon. To have it all dragged out into the open, for it to end like that, for it to end *then*, had to have been embarrassing and distracting. But you played through it without complaint, carrying it all on your shoulders, and carrying your teammates, too. The Mavericks lost in five games, but that wasn't your fault.

This guy is playing a little soft. Unbelievable. Especially coming from someone like Webber, who had a documented history, going back to his freshman year at Michigan, of shrinking in big moments.

A few months later, I got a chance to talk to you about it. You told me I had it wrong, at least a little bit. You said it was good that the situation with Taylor happened when it did.

"I was able to concentrate on the stuff that I love to do, which is playing basketball. In the morning for an hour in shootaround and at night for two and a half hours. I could escape a little bit, if you want. I could get away from it a little bit, see the guys and hang out with the guys in the locker room, and they talked to me and handled me like everything was normal. I think that was important for me, that the guys were great and supportive."

After it was over, you took your parents and your sister and her husband and their kids to the beach. They had questions, so you told them about everything that had happened. You went back to Germany and there were more questions. You had a press conference and told the assembled reporters about everything that had happened. You got through it, just like you always had.

This guy is playing a little soft.

Everything you wanted was so close. It would take one more season—notable only for the trades that brought in key contributors Shawn Marion, Caron Butler, Brendan Haywood, and DeShawn Stevenson—before you could get there, both on the court and off. But even when we talked in 2009, there was a peace about you, like you knew, like you had seen it and just had to wait until it was time. Just had to be patient for a little while longer.

Because it was coming. A championship. A family.

It was coming.

It was almost there.

It was time.

9

And I Am Coming Home to You
If It's the Last Thing That I Do

A group of us watched Game 6 of the 2011 Finals at Joe's house in Oak Cliff, southwest of downtown. It was a bit strange, because we hadn't watched any of the other games there and, in fact, I had never even been there. But it was appropriate, too, because Isaac had always liked Joe—he yelled a lot when he got excited—and Joe, of course, had been a big part of 2006. He was our good luck charm in the deciding game against the Spurs, power-smoking on Eric's porch. It was the right spot to see you and the Mavs (finally win).

No one wanted to say those words out loud or even see them next to each other, not until was done. That fucking parade route from 2006 hung over everything. So much had felt cursed since then: 2006 and 2007, obviously, but every other season had some sort of only-in-Dallas type of self-inflicted kick in the jeans. In 2010, the Mavs had gone into the playoffs as the No. 2 seed in the Western Conference—and lost in six games against the Spurs, despite you shooting like you were in an empty gym. That loss didn't hurt as much; we were becoming numb. And it really seemed like you were destined to join Charles Barkley and Karl Malone on the list of the

best players never to win a ring. You turned thirty-two a couple of months after the season ended. Time was running out.

Even earlier in this unexpected run, in fact, there had been a hint of that self-sabotage, when Portland's Brandon Roy led a big comeback in the third game of the opening round, a twentysomething-point second-half lead becoming another disastrous loss followed by every talking head and national beat writer and blogger harmonizing on the playoff-classic slow jam, "Same Old Mavs."

Beating Kobe Bryant and the Lakers—*sweeping* Kobe Bryant and the Lakers—helped, and so did taking down Oklahoma City in the Western Conference finals, still with its Kevin Durant-Russell Westbrook-James Harden triumvirate, even if that group of three future MVPs, only in its second season together, had a slight whiff of *just happy to be there*. But it wasn't until the Miami series that it felt different. Only then did it feel like we were out of reach of the ghosts. Your layup that finished off a giant run that salvaged Game 2 was through-the-looking-glass business, shot like an art film, a speck of blue on a white-sand beach.

Still, it was hard to say "The Mavs are going to win" out loud, even alone, as if it might summon the bogeyman. No one wanted that anguish again, to invite it over the threshold willingly, to set themselves up for it. Guards were up all over town. And they were definitely still up at Joe's house, even though it was more or less set up as a victory party. We had been let down so many times, maybe we didn't believe in the Mavs anymore. But we hadn't stopped believing in you yet. Couldn't.

⊕ ⊕ ⊕

You sprained your right knee in a December 27 game against the Thunder, after landing on it awkwardly. It was early in the second quarter and Serge Ibaka had fouled you on a fadeaway, and you tumbled backward. "It was just a scary play," you said after.

You had only missed thirty-one games in thirteen seasons, but you would miss the next nine, your longest stretch in street clothes by far. (The only benefit of this time was that it gave you occasion to pop onto the Fox Southwest broadcast during a home game against the Toronto Raptors. When Tyson Chandler finished off a lob from Jason Kidd, you screamed into your microphone, "*Take dat witchu!*" and then we wanted you on the call for every game after that.) You'd turned and twisted your ankles like pipe cleaners, like your feet had been attached in a rush and imperfectly, but you'd always come back sooner than expected, quicker than most, sometimes missing no time at all.

But this wasn't the same. Your ankles were legendary, but your knees didn't have the same reputation. You'd famously hurt the left one during the 2003 Western Conference finals and hadn't been able to recover in time to make a difference, and that was when you were younger, hundreds of games earlier. After an athlete turns thirty, you never know what injury to which body part will be the one that ends his career, or at least ends the good part of it. You were thirty-two.

When you went down against the Thunder, you were averaging 24.5 points and 7.6 rebounds on frankly insane 54.5 percent

shooting, ridiculous for a jump shooter. The Mavericks were 24–5 and in the conversation regarding title contention—after being ignored for most of three seasons—while you were a dark-horse MVP candidate. Or whatever is darker than a dark horse. Like midnight shadows had conspired to form the faintest outline of a horse under a moonless sky. But still, it was happening.

It was a long way from where things stood in the fall, when you had been forsaken. Before the season, Tom Ziller, then of AOL's then-wonderful, now-defunct FanHouse, wrote, "The Mavs' season depends on [second-year guard Rodrigue] Beaubois bursting out and coach Rick Carlisle using him properly. Beaubois is the only hope." John Hollinger, writing for ESPN, said that any chance the Mavs had of "winning anything important" depended on Beaubois. But the French guard would miss most of the season with a broken foot, come back briefly, then miss all of the playoffs. And how could he be the only hope when you were still around? I'm not picking on Ziller or Hollinger, because they weren't the only ones who voiced that opinion. Even fans had taken to worshipping false idols. And why? At best, you were being taken for granted. Mostly it felt like you had been forgotten.

But you had forced your way back into everyone's consciousness—and then you fell. The Mavs slumped with you out, which strengthened your MVP case but caused talk of title contention to take a hit that it never quite recovered from. Especially after what happened in Milwaukee, in your third missed game: forward Caron Butler tore his right patella tendon, which led to season-ending

surgery. Butler was a few years removed from his days as an All-Star with the Wizards, but he was a steady fifteen-per-game scorer and eased the team's reliance on you; he'd had thirty the game before he went down. The Mavs were able to replace Butler's production by bringing in Corey Brewer and Peja Stojaković, your old Kings nemesis, and moving Shawn Marion into the starting lineup. In fact, the team may have been better. Over a month, from January 22 through March 4, the Mavs won eighteen games and lost just once, on the way to an eleventh consecutive season with fifty or more wins.[32]

But no one around the league put much stock in it. All of it was written off as just the usual regular-season routine and they'd seen enough of that before. All this time later and it was still like you were playing in a bright yellow "We Believe!" Warriors shirt.

No one could see beyond the surface. Sure, your running mate was still Jason Terry, and that hadn't worked out yet. But the roster that had been quietly assembled over the previous three seasons was quite different apart from the two of you, much more like the 2003 team, built on veteran players who knew their roles and didn't try to do more and never did less—Kidd, Marion, Tyson Chandler, Stojaković, DeShawn Stevenson, Brian Cardinal.

When did you know that these guys were different?

⊕   ⊕   ⊕

---

32. Only the third team to do that since the NBA went to an eighty-two-game schedule in 1967.

In an April 1 *New York Times* column ostensibly about Chicago Bulls guard Derrick Rose's MVP chances, Neil Paine, an analyst at Basketball-Reference.com, wrote that you had "carried the Mavericks, but he also carries the stigma of an embarrassing playoff flameout as MVP in 2007." It was a drive-by.

Except for a short shooting slump at the end of March—Cuban said at the time, somewhat prophetically, "I'm glad he's having a tough spot now so he can get those games out of the way"—you were as good as ever.[33] But no one was paying attention, and when they were, it was only to dismiss you and the team's chances. It was difficult to blame them. The Mavs had won *one* playoff series since the 2006 Western Conference finals. Every chance the team had to make a statement, it ended up being: *Ah, fuck. Not again.*

On the last day of March, on a Thursday night TNT game, the defending-champion Lakers smoked the Mavs by twenty-eight, despite your twenty-seven and thirteen. Eddie Sefko, then the Mavs beat writer for the *Dallas Morning News*, wrote that "their apparent collision course with the Lakers in the second round of the playoffs—assuming the Mavericks make it that far—has disaster written all over it, based on the events of the last few weeks." It gave Lakers coach (and notorious shit-talker) Phil Jackson a chance to say things about you like, "You know he can shoot his way out of a wheelchair," and "This guy's going to play forever but he definitely has a limited gait."

---

33. Even with that tough spot, you had 24.6 points and 7.9 rebounds on 51.6 percent shooting in 16 March games.

The Lakers game was the first of four straight losses. A few nights later, after you went five of twelve for just sixteen points in a loss to the Portland Trail Blazers, the Mavs' likely first-round opponent, Jennifer Floyd Engel of Fort Worth's *Star-Telegram* wrote: "Nothing died Sunday in Portland, despite contrary reports. Nothing that was ever real anyway. What we witnessed with LaMarcus Aldridge and his Trail Blazers slapping an already wobbly Dallas Mavericks bunch around was just further indicators of a team limping through another April for another date with yet another premature postseason ejection. The Mavs are not contenders for anything of weight." Later, she added, "This is an aging team trying to slap together one last run for Dirk Nowitzki—except road trips like this latest seem to illustrate how unlikely that actually would be."

You wrote it off as the result of a long road trip, maintaining that the Mavs were "a dangerous team." Not that anyone agreed with you. Denver coach George Karl took the unusual step—but not all that out of character for a Noted Dickhead™ like Karl—of saying that he wanted to play the Mavericks in the first round. Matt Barnes, formerly of the Warriors, then with the Lakers, said, "In Golden State, we showed how to beat Dallas. You get in there and take it right to their chin and they back down. I don't see anything has changed since then, so hopefully we will see them again." And maybe even your teammates didn't agree at the moment. Frustrations came to a head in a win over the Clippers. Terry got into an argument with guard J.J. Barea that turned into a confrontation with Carlisle.

But you were still calm about it all: "Maybe this is the game we

needed to kind of get some stuff out and refocus and play with each other and fight with each other," you said after the game, in which you had a season-high seven assists. "That's what it's going to take in the playoffs. We've got to leave it all on the court, and all five guys got to be out there on a string and really fight, because if you look at the first-round matchup, it's going to be tough whoever we see. We're only going to win if we play hard together."

You beat Phoenix next and completed a season-ending four-game winning streak with an overtime victory in Houston (you had twenty-three and twelve) and then a blowout win over Chris Paul and New Orleans (you put up thirty-two points in thirty-one minutes, your highest scoring total in almost a month).

And then it was playoff time. Mavs versus Blazers. Tensions were higher than they'd ever been, and expectations were almost nonexistent.

"It should be a fun run," you said.

⊕   ⊕   ⊕

A few days before the end of the season, Rick Carlisle told Dwain Price of the *Star-Telegram* about the first time he saw you, back when he was an assistant coach for the Indiana Pacers, under Larry Bird. They were watching a tape of your performance at the Nike Hoop Summit in San Antonio.

"Larry said this guy is going to be an unbelievable player just because of how he moved, how he ran, his ability to shoot the ball, he

had a good feel for the game. You knew he could be a game-changing type guy. Back then we all knew he was going to be a tremendous player."

The team finished with fifty-seven wins, its most since 2007, and tied for the best road record (28–13). But you'd won fifty-five the previous season, won the Southwest Division, and didn't even make it to May, losing in the first round to the seventh-seeded Spurs. And that was with a healthy Caron Butler. The Mavs may have survived just fine without Butler in the second half of the season, but there wasn't much faith that would continue in the playoffs. The team's full name had become the Dallas Mavericks Who Have Won One Playoff Series Since Being Up 2–0 against Miami in the 2006 Finals. In a debate among sportswriters in the Tribune chain, all four—Ira Winderman of the *Sun-Sentinel*, K.C. Johnson of the *Chicago Tribune*, Zach McCann of the *Orlando Sentinel*, and Lisa Dillman from the *Los Angeles Times*—picked Portland to upset you guys. McCann said the Blazers were "Dirk-stoppers." They weren't alone. Six of twelve ESPN experts predicted a Portland win, and the other six didn't expect Dallas to go any further.

No one believed in the Mavs, which mostly meant no one believed in you. But your teammates did.

"Look what he does every night," Brendan Haywood said. "He's the type of guy that his game was never built on athleticism. It's built on skill, so guys like that can play longer and play at a higher level for a long period of time."

For your part, you weren't worried about Portland. You took

the Blazers seriously, but at this point, it wasn't about first-round victories. "We're playing for championships," you said. "That's really the only goal. I don't know if we have something to prove. If we don't win a championship, it's another disappointing season."

In Game 1, you scored twelve straight in the fourth quarter, even though you'd been struggling with your shot all game. "Dirk came alive," Blazers center Marcus Camby marveled. You finished with twenty-eight points, eighteen in the final quarter, in an 89–81 win.

Game 2, you were better, capping your thirty-three-point night with the last eleven of the game, a 101–89 win. There was a wave of *OK, maybe this* is *different* stories. And then:

(oh no)

You had twenty-five points and nine rebounds in a Game 3 loss. The last time the Mavs and Blazers had met in the playoffs, in 2003, you guys had gone up 3–0 before the Blazers rallied to force a seventh game. So at least *that* wouldn't happen this time. And then:

(oh no no no)

In Game 4, the Mavs were up twenty-three points with a minute left in the third quarter. You'd end up losing by two.

Brandon Roy—a.k.a. Andy Cleft, method actor—had eighteen in fourth, twenty-two in the second half. With Roy chipping away at the lead, even on knees meant for the stage not for pull-up jumpers,

you looked to have wrested control of the game back from him with 2:16 left, when you hit a driving shot and drew a foul, a potential three-point play that would have put the Mavs up nine. But you were called for an offensive foul instead and Portland scored twelve seconds later to make it 80–76 and all those *OK maybe this* is *different* stories were just kindling on the fire. The Mavs only scored two more points. It wasn't Portland in 2003. It was worse. It was Miami in 2006.

"This is definitely up there with the most frustrating losses," you said.

Maybe you would have pressed too hard before, tried to do too much. Every sin of the past was dredged up between Games 4 and 5, every meltdown and mistake. Maybe in 2008 or 2009 you would have tried to silence the doubters with every eighteen-footer. But, like you said, it was about winning a championship. It was necessary to get past Portland to do so. That was all. That was the only point to make.

You were the first to speak in the locker room after Game 4, even before Carlisle, and then you led by example. You scored twenty-five points in a Game 5 win that was decided in the third quarter, when you had eleven points in a 15–5 run. "The West is wide open," you said. "That's what you see now in the playoffs. Teams can be beaten." In a way, the losses had given you more confidence: if others could do it, why not the Mavs? Why not you? "No team really looks unbeatable right now, so we've just got to keep on plugging, keep on fighting, and hopefully get a big win on Thursday and go from there."

You made sure that happened, with thirty-three points,[34] setting the mood in the second quarter. Rookie Chris Johnson fouled you, leading to a three-point play, then got up in your face. On the next Portland possession, Johnson was called for a flagrant foul on you.

"Toughness doesn't always mean throwing a punch back or doing something like that," Tyson Chandler said. "It means getting back up and going at them even tougher when you're frustrated. Dirk got up, and instead of getting in some confrontation, he said, OK, I'm gonna punish you [on the court]. And that's the way we've got to do it." It's exactly how your hero Scottie Pippen handled the Detroit Pistons when the Chicago Bulls finally got past the Bad Boys in 1991. He took the hits and kept going, and that's when the Pistons knew they were finished. So maybe we should have known right then where this was headed.

And do you remember what happened as the game ended? The Portland fans yelled for you to beat L.A.

"Nobody knows what's going to happen against the Lakers in the second round," Eddie Sefko wrote. "But it's going to be the type of stage Nowitzki deserves. He'll be going against Kobe Bryant and the national media will be dissecting his game. Based on what happened against the Blazers, Nowitzki is ready."

You were confident, but cautious.

"We'll have our hands full," you said.

---

34. Shooting 11–17 from the floor and a perfect 11–11 from the line, along with 11 rebounds and 4 assists.

⊕ ⊕ ⊕

The 2010–11 season was an important one for me and Isaac, and still would be the most important one, regardless of how it ended. His mom and I split up in March 2010, after a few months of headed that way quickly, after a couple of years of headed that way slowly, and officially divorced in June 2010—just when the NBA offseason was beginning, not that I could have been bothered to notice.

Isaac and I had found a new place, but we lived there without any furniture except for our beds for a few months, since what I had was being used to stage the house that I was still paying a mortgage on, which was lingering on the market rather uncomfortably. I had at least gotten a hundred dollars knocked off rent by using my status as a newly divorced father—I didn't have to tell Isaac to look especially forlorn or fake anything, just quietly nod my head in his direction while negotiating. But it wasn't easy. We spent most of our time together, in the beginning, anyway, playing *Lego Star Wars* on the old desktop computer in his room, sharing the keyboard, me hunched over on a little plastic chair from IKEA made for toddlers.

Eventually, we transitioned to basketball in the driveway. He had always been interested, and I'd encouraged that by modifying his Little Tykes hoop into something slightly more realistic by inserting a broom handle between the backboard and the base and taping it all together. And I was a coach on his YMCA team.[35] But now he

---

35. I started as an assistant and in a year or so became the head coach, a

was *interested*. We went to visit my parents in Waco, and while there I had fallen ill, nothing serious, just enough where I had to lie on the couch and watch the HBO documentary about Magic Johnson and Larry Bird. Isaac lay next to me and asked questions; by the end, he was in—on basketball and the way those two played it.

We had gone to a couple of games together and watched a few more, and he could stay invested for a half, maybe three quarters, very, very occasionally all the way through. (Josh Howard was his favorite player, so far as he had one, sorry.) But when the 2010–11 season began, he was intensely focused, vigilant. He had questions and comments, opinions. If there wasn't a game on, we were in the driveway playing one of our own, usually HORSE to compensate for the height and age difference.

It was our first season on our own, and his first season really watching basketball—*getting* basketball—and all of it saved us a little. He loved me, he loves me, but until then Isaac had turned to his mother for everything important, and just about everything else, too. We didn't have that bond they had already developed, a hidden language, secret to them.

But now we were getting there, shot by shot, game by game.

⊕   ⊕   ⊕

---

position I held until he was in high school. My "system" was pretty simple: play as hard as you can on defense and you can do whatever you want on offense.

Other teams, historically, had the Mavs' number, and in your era there were the Kings, at least at the beginning, and the Spurs always. But none of them could match the Lakers' grip on the team's psyche (and that of its fans as well), and it went back almost to the very beginning of the franchise.

The Mavs' first playoff appearance[36] in 1984 ended in the second round in Los Angeles, one game after Derek Harper mistakenly dribbled out the clock in a tie game. They were knocked out by L.A. in 1986, and again in 1988, in the team's first trip to the Western Conference finals. After losing in seven, the Mavs wouldn't win another playoff game until 2001. They went from March 1990 to December 2003 without winning on the road against the Lakers. In 1997, in Los Angeles, the Mavs set an NBA record by scoring just two points in the third quarter, a pair of Harper free throws with 1:51 remaining; they had been up 51–37 at halftime and would go on to lose 87–80. In December 2002, when you guys were 17–1, on the way to winning sixty games, you blew a twenty-seven-point fourth-quarter lead at the Staples Center. There was the debacle to open the 2003–04 season, when looking overmatched against the Shaq-and-Kobe Lakers was somehow overshadowed by the debut (and farewell) of the trash-bag uniforms. In 2005, Bryant outscored the Mavericks on his own through three quarters, 62–61.

---

36. This is the one that featured the legendary Moody Madness game: the deciding Game 5 of the opening-round series versus the Seattle Supersonics had to be moved to SMU's Moody Coliseum (capacity: 9,007), about half the size of Reunion Arena (18,190), because of a scheduling conflict. The Mavs won 105–104 in overtime.

I know you know all this. But we have to go through it together. It's part of the journey.

Beyond all of that, if that wasn't more than enough, the version of the Lakers you were about to face were the defending NBA champions and had given you and the team perhaps your worst loss of the season about a month earlier, despite a typically all-caps performance by you. It had always been that way, since you joined the league. Bryant was two months younger than you, but he already had five championship rings.

"We got to go for it in Game 1 and Game 2 and let it all hang out," you said before the series. "You got to go for it in the first one. That's how we're going to approach it. You never want to trail in a series, so Game 1 is big. We got to learn from that [the last regular season game in L.A.]. They're going to try to do the same thing Portland did and that's being physical. We can't let that bother us. We can't lose our composure like we did in the last game there. We got to fight through that stuff."

Can I tell you something? I didn't think you could beat the Lakers, or we could beat the Lakers, or the Mavs could beat the Lakers. However you want to put it.

I just couldn't believe.

I wasn't alone.

"Not a lot of people picked us to win this series," you said after Game 6 in Portland, "and not a lot of people are going to pick us to win the next series." All fourteen ESPN experts, in fact, picked the Lakers.

Charles Barkley knew you could win. He had been a fan since he saw you play when you faced his all-star Nike team as a teenager in Germany. He had also often been critical, wanting you to take over more, be more aggressive, stop taking shit from anyone. Be more like Charles Barkley, in other words. But he had no qualms picking the Mavs to advance in six, almost solely because of No. 41. "In all my thirty years around the NBA, Dirk Nowitzki has the most unique game. He's a seven-foot guy who can shoot threes, he can put it on the floor, and I know Pau Gasol and Andrew Bynum have zero chance."

Barkley expanded on his comments in an interview with the *Dallas Morning News'* Tim Cowlishaw, saying this was the best Mavs team he had seen, better than 2006 or 2007.

"I don't think anyone in the world can guard Dirk Nowitzki, but I know for sure those people can't."

You proved his point in Game 1 in Los Angeles, scoring eleven points in the fourth quarter and four in the final forty seconds, including a pair of free throws with 19.5 left to give the Mavs their first lead of the game, after being down by sixteen in the third quarter.

"We're mentally tougher than we have been," you said. "It showed after the meltdown in Portland, coming back and winning two games when everybody said we were dead. We're a lot of veteran guys who have been around a lot in this league."

After Game 1, the results of the MVP vote were announced. Derrick Rose had won, unsurprisingly. But you finished a respectable

sixth.[37] Maybe the team's dismal 2–7 record in the nine games you missed reminded voters of your value.

The Lakers gave up on Gasol and Lamar Odom trying to check you, putting the soon-to-be-former Ron Artest[38] on you instead. The six-foot-seven forward was quicker and more physical, and while that had worked for Miami in 2006 and Golden State in 2007, that wasn't a problem for you by then, was it? Not anymore. You had twenty-four points, fifteen in the first half on fadeaways, shooting right over your defender's head, your one-knee-up form starting to become synonymous with this run. The Mavs won 93–81, taking both games in L.A.

"We talked about it and this series is far from over," you said. You'd evolved into the ideal hero in a horror movie, never for a second believing the killer was dead. "I've been around a long time. I've been up 2-0 before and ended up losing the series. And I've been down 2-0, lost both games to Houston a couple of years ago, and came back and won Game 7. So we've seen a lot of things happen in this league."

You were only getting better. In Game 3, the Lakers, running out of ideas, tried a supersized lineup featuring Odom, Gasol, and Bynum, all over six foot ten. You simply stepped further out, hitting

---

37. You finished behind Rose, Dwight Howard, LeBron James, Bryant, and Kevin Durant, earning five second-place votes, three thirds, eleven fourths, and thirty fifth-place votes.

38. He would legally change his name to Metta World Peace in September.

four of five threes, and scoring thirty-two points—eighteen in the first half and four in the last 2:40 of the game.

The biggest two came on a running lefty hook with 1:39 remaining, you flipping it in over two defenders. You ran back up the court with your sneer-smile and the lead and it started to sink in that this was really happening, that you were *making* this happen, would not let it *not* happen.

"Just about everything that happened down the stretch was a direct result of him either scoring the ball or making a play to get somebody a shot or make a pass for an assist for a three or whatever it was," Carlisle said.

And people could see what you were doing. "Now he takes the shots he wants to take 95 percent of the time," Hall of Famer Kevin McHale said. He had been around during training camp, visiting Carlisle, his old Celtics teammate. "Prior, the opposing defense won that battle more often." That was more perception than reality, but at least the perception was changing.

You, however, were understandably still cautious, at least off the court. "We're not good enough to relax or take the pedal off the metal. You don't want to ever give a champion life, so hopefully we can have the same effort and the same crowd and a great game on Sunday."

You said you had seen a lot of things happen in this league, but you meant *to you*, mostly. The possibility of making negative history—losing after being up 3–0—was still out there, and if anyone could inflict that on you, it was the Lakers. "I don't want to be the first one," you said. Not again.

But you wouldn't be.

Game 4 was a blowout. A *blowout*. A BLOWOUT. The Mavs beat the Lakers 122–86, and honestly it wasn't even that close. Isaac and I watched sitting on the floor of our rented house, him bouncing up with every good play, at some point taking his shirt off—he was seven and he did that back then when he got excited, like his enthusiasm could not be restrained by clothes. The team went twenty of thirty-two from three—Terry had nine of them and Stojakovic went six for six—and you didn't have to do much. After averaging 27.6 over the first nine games of the playoffs, you had an efficient seventeen points (on 7–11 shooting, along with seven rebounds and four assists)—but were a team-high +37 for the game.

"I'm going to enjoy this for a day," you said. "I think I'm gonna have some pizza and cheat on my diet." Maybe you had a beer, too. Maybe you thought about those nights out with Steve.

⊕   ⊕   ⊕

Did you know what happened to Robert "Tractor" Traylor?

On May 11, three days after you swept the Lakers, Traylor—the big man infamously traded for you in the 1998 draft—was found dead on the floor of his beachside apartment in San Juan, Puerto Rico, where he had been playing for the Vaqueros de Bayamón.

San Juan was the last stop on his basketball odyssey. After seven years in the NBA—with the Milwaukee Bucks, Cleveland Cavaliers, both the Charlotte and New Orleans Hornets, and the Cavaliers

again—Traylor played in Spain, Puerto Rico, Turkey, Italy, Puerto Rico (again), Mexico, and Puerto Rico (again again). He was out injured at the time of his death. He had been on the phone with his wife, Raye, in Chicago, when the call abruptly cut off. He apparently had a heart attack.

Traylor averaged 4.8 points and 3.7 rebounds in 438 NBA games. He'd had surgery on his aorta in 2005, and that had caused NBA teams to look elsewhere and started his roaming.

"He was very friendly," the Vaqueros' manager, Jose Carlos Perez, said after Traylor was found in his apartment. "He got along with everyone. The fans loved him, idolized him."

Traylor never asked to be the answer to a trivia question, a slide in an online gallery, a footnote. It might have been easier if it had been the other way around, if he had become the legend, the all-time great, the folk hero, and you had to go back to Europe in 2005, if you'd had to fall back on your fallback plan, even if it meant you had to go back to playing small-time club ball in Würzburg and working for your family's house painting business, getting up shots after work in the tiny gym because you loved it, if for no other reason. You were built for it.

"I've thought a lot about this, like why is he the way that he is?" Jeff "Skin" Wade, one of the Mavs' broadcasters, told me a couple of months after you retired. "One of the unique things about his situation is, and he's not a sad person, but he definitely has the stereotypical German fatalistic thing in some regard, right? But he's very hardworking and very working-class, very team-oriented. There's

these sort of European sensibilities that aren't like the capitalistic sensibilities. The things Dirk grew up wanting and desiring are so at odds with what the other NBA players—the way they looked at the game and what it could be for him. His version is very idealized. It's hard to idealize something when this is your only chance to make it. And so I think Dirk's sensibility is, you know, basketball greatness, it's cool and all of these things, but I think Dirk could have gone and done a blue-collar job or got an education, whatever."

It's hard to imagine you as the world's tallest house painter. But it's not impossible.

⊕ ⊕ ⊕

Before the season, in July, the Mavericks traded for Tyson Chandler, swapping Erick Dampier (prayer hands emoji), Eddie Najera, and Matt Carroll for the former No. 2 pick in the 2001 draft. He'd killed you guys as a member of the New Orleans Hornets in 2008, averaging eleven rebounds a game and catching roughly 4,027 lobs from Chris Paul. I vividly remember when I snuck away from a Passover Seder to catch the first game of the Mavs-Hornets first-round series and feeling like Chandler was playing SlamBall. He always seemed to be airborne.

The Hornets traded him to Oklahoma City in 2009, but the Thunder's team doctors had decided his left big toe was an injury risk and called off the deal. He went to Charlotte in the offseason, where his left foot did indeed cause him to miss twenty-nine games.

It looked like the Thunder doctors were right. The Mavs brought him in to back up Brendan Haywood, a key step in building a championship roster around you, but only in retrospect. It was a very low-stakes deal at the time. That changed when the season began. Chandler immediately became a starter and the focal point of your defense, playing in seventy-four games, starting all of them, averaging ten points and just under ten rebounds, and always getting your back.

He'd faced you plenty of times over the years, but still didn't know you very well. The accent threw him off. "I felt like he was really European and not Americanized in any way," he'd tell me later. But when he got a chance to hear more of what you said instead of how you said it, he saw it differently. "He's a super-intelligent dude and has a grasp on the culture and what's going on and is just a funny dude, always cracking jokes. I didn't realize he listened to so much hip-hop. All the basketball stuff was exactly what I expected."

All the basketball stuff: that had gotten you guys to the Western Conference finals, almost all the way back.

"Especially going through 2006, I think Dirk realized that we had a complete team and this was his one real shot to really go after it, and he did that," Chandler told me in 2019. "He was so locked in that entire season and especially when it came to the playoffs. There was such an intensity around him. He's not on intense person, but you felt it. I felt like every other guy, you know, you got to do your part. Look at this man, look at what he's doing, look at how he's driving himself. You just have to do your part.

"I remember that time of year, I wanted it so bad for myself and I wanted it just as bad for him, because I was a fan of his. I watched him lose in that Finals. I watched Miami celebrate on that floor. I watched him walk off. I watched all those things and so I understood where he was at, his head, mentally, and I wanted to help him get past that hurdle. I'd never seen anybody like that in my career. He was just in such a zone.

"I remember me and DeShawn Stevenson, we were watching— we had shootaround and it was 9:00 in the morning or whatever, and I remember that Dirk had a full sweat. Oklahoma City was walking off the court and me and DeShawn were like, *We just got to get this man there. If we can get him there, I can't see nobody beating him this year, how locked in he is, the type of player he is. We just got to get him there. He'll close the deal if we get him there. That's our job.* I honestly didn't care who was in the NBA. I'm like, *You're not beating this guy. He has too many weapons.*"

The Thunder were not without weapons of their own, and their weapons had weapons. They had Kevin Durant, Russell Westbrook, and James Harden—all of whom would go on to win MVP trophies within the decade—plus Serge Ibaka and Kendrick Perkins, who had won a title with Boston in 2008. But all Dallas needed was you. You scored 48 points in Game 1 on 12–15 shooting and an insane twenty-four of twenty-four on free throws (setting an NBA record for most made without a miss), along with six rebounds, four assists, and four blocks.

That set the tone for a five-game series in which you'd average

more than thirty-two points; there was no letdown, no exhale after sweeping the Lakers. The angles on your shots got increasingly ridiculous. More often than not, at the moment of release, it looked like you were inside a panel of a comic strip and had slipped on a banana peel. Your only actual slip was in Game 3: you had seven turnovers and only eighteen points on 7–21 shooting. But even then, you came through when it mattered, scoring ten points in the fourth and hitting a classic off-balance runner around the five-minute mark with the lead shrinking, and an eleven-foot jumper with under a minute left to put the Mavs up six. Chandler did his part, making all of his shots and pulling in fifteen rebounds.

The series was much closer than the 4–1 result suggests now. The Thunder won Game 2 on the road and was poised to win Game 4, up fifteen with five minutes left, until the Mavs stormed back to win in overtime behind twelve points from you and strong defense from the rest of the team, playoff experience winning out. So, no, it wasn't easy. But after five years and more than a full career's worth of misfortune, you had made it back to the Finals, back to Miami. Not that you cared who you were playing.

"Really, after '06, we were so disappointed with Miami and we would love to get a chance again, but then '07 happened," you told me after you retired. "We won seventy games. We didn't get back. Then we did the [Kidd] trade, '08, I think we lose early. '09, lose to Denver. By the time we finally got back to the Finals in '11, I would have played a team from Siberia or something.

"Honestly, after '06 and '07, I thought we're going to the Finals

for years here on out. After you go to the Finals one year, you win seventy games the next, you're thinking, hey, we're a great team and we're going to be here the next couple of years. And then it's kind of taken away from me, like that. So it was a battle for us to even make it back in '11 and it was, to us, it was a great side thing that we happened to play Miami again. But for me, I wanted to have tunnel vision. Who knows? It might be your last shot at getting that thing and getting to the Finals. I would have played any team in the world."

Let me sum up my own feelings on the matter quickly: I wanted to beat the motherfucking Heat.

Narratively, besides you (and Jason Terry) seeking redemption for what happened against Miami in 2006, there was the idea of the Mavs, carried on the back of their franchise player, going up against a super team, the so-called Heatles, with LeBron James and Chris Bosh joining their fellow member of the 2003 draft class, The Hated Dwyane Wade. LeBron had become a villain in the league for the first time, after announcing he was leaving Cleveland via a TV special broadcast live on ESPN called *The Decision*. (He infamously said he was "taking his talents to South Beach.") Dallas vs. Miami was David vs. Goliath, old vs. new, European socialism vs. the height of American capitalism—however you wanted to frame it. There were plot holes in all of these stories, but that didn't mean they weren't great stories.

The narrative was almost impossible to resist. It all felt familiar.

In 2006: after taking down a longtime foe (the Spurs), you scored fifty against Phoenix in the Western Conference finals, leading to a faceoff with the Miami Heat.

In 2011: after taking down a longtime foe (the Lakers), you scored forty-eight against Oklahoma City in the Western Conference finals, leading to a faceoff with the Miami Heat.

But you weren't thinking about parallels or anything else.

"There's been a lot made of what's my legacy without it, with it," you said about a potential championship before Game 1. "I'm trying to be on the best team. I'm trying to win it for this organization and for the owner and for myself and for the team. I'm not worried about my legacy without the ring or with the ring. I'm living in the moment. We have another chance, and I'm going for it. We can talk about my legacy once my career is over. I'm really just focused."

In the runup to Game 1, Larry Bird said that he was "honored" to be compared to you. And your opponents, at least before things got started, paid you the proper respect. Wade and James wouldn't remain quite so reverent as the series wore on. James was still in his one and only season in a villain role, a slight heel turn that never completely fit.

James: "The things he's able to do, forced to a bad shot. It looks like a bad shot if you don't know his game. One-legged fadeaways off the glass, pull-up fadeaways off the dribble. He's a great player."

Bosh: "He'll hit enough how-did-he-do-it shots, but you have to limit his easy buckets. He practices awkward shots."

Wade: "Obviously, his shot-making ability is one of the best this league has seen. But I think what he's gotten better at is taking over games in the fourth quarter."

Before Game 1, MediaTakeOut reported that you and your

girlfriend, Jessica Olsson, had gotten engaged, and the Dallas media had picked up on the story. You and Jessica hadn't even been in public much, so it was an unexpected intrusion, your personal life once again making a surprise appearance during a playoff run. But you stayed focused. Warming up, you went through your routine same as always, circling around the key shooting one-legged fadeaways off your left foot, then back around with your right. There were celebrities at courtside—Ludacris, Jimmy Buffett, Timbaland, Gloria Estefan, Jerry Bruckheimer—but that didn't matter either.

And then it began.

Wade and Udonis Haslem were the only holdovers from the Heat's 2006 title team, but Game 1 looked pretty similar to where that series left off, Haslem hounding you into a poor shooting night and defeat. At one point, you dribbled the ball off your knee and out of bounds.

"We all know Udonis Haslem is a good defender, probably one of the best in the league," you said, generously. The loss made it five in a row in the Finals, five in a row to Miami. You finished with a game-high twenty-seven (you were 12–12 from the line) and you had twelve in the fourth quarter, including six points in the last three minutes. But it was too late. Worse, you tore a tendon in the tip of your left middle finger trying to strip Bosh late in the game. Brian Cardinal suggested you cut off the end of the finger at the knuckle, like San Francisco 49ers safety Ronnie Lott infamously (and regrettably) did to keep playing in the 1980s.

You wouldn't have to do anything that drastic, but the finger

did pose a problem. It was on your nonshooting hand, but you did like to go left, dribbling hard to get into your shot or to keep going all the way to the rim. You worked on the practice court between games with Holger, to see what you needed to do to compensate, what you could and couldn't do.

"Hey, Rondo played with one arm, so he might be able to play with nine fingers," Holger said, referencing the game earlier that postseason in the Eastern Conference semifinals when Celtics point guard Rajon Rondo kept playing after the training staff popped his dislocated left elbow back into place.

Jet said, "I think Dirk can shoot the ball with his eyes closed and no hands, if he had to, especially in a game of this magnitude."

You weren't overly concerned, a common reaction to every bit of trouble you had encountered that postseason. You could have been hit by a car walking into the arena and you would have just said, "Obviously, it's going to affect my movement a little bit." Or what you said about your finger:

"I think once the game starts, the adrenaline starts flowing, I don't think it will really slow me down much."

You had to wear a splint the rest of the series, and Casey Smith, the head trainer, had made it as small as possible. But for the bulk of Game 2, it seemed like it wouldn't have mattered if your arm was in a sling. You could have had a full cast on and stopped along the sideline to have Jimmy Buffett sign it, something like, "To a Würzburger in paradise, ha ha ha, Jimmy," and it wouldn't have changed much. The Heat were on their way to a win and a 2–0 series lead.

Wade hit a three-pointer with 7:14 remaining to put the Heat up fifteen, holding the follow-through like he was Sidney Deane in *White Men Can't Jump* while he was all but sitting on the Mavs' bench, then celebrated with James as they walked back up the sideline. It wasn't exactly egregious, but it was enough to fire up you and the other Mavs.[39]

What did Carlisle tell you to do?

Prove that the game wasn't over.

What did Terry say?

"There's no way we're going out like this."

The Mavs went on a 22-5 run to close the game and win 95–93. Miami had been 9-0 at home in the playoffs prior to that. You scored the final nine points, the last two on a spinning *left*-handed layup, *yessir*, with 3.6 seconds remaining. The last basket was a painting, a solitary missionary in royal blue set against a sea of white. It was the reverse of Game 3 in 2006, almost exactly. Not only did you prevail this time, but you showed how much you had grown. You put the team up 93–90 with a wide-open three with 26.7 seconds left—then Heat guard Mario Chalmers tied it two seconds later, off the inbounds pass, because Terry had lost him trying to anticipate a pass to Wade and left him free. You yelled at him during the ensuing timeout ("We love each other," you said later. "We also argue a lot.")

---

39. Remember that James and Wade got into a semantics argument with reporters over the word "celebration"? "A celebration is confetti," Wade said. "A celebration is champagne. There was no celebration."

but then you did something you might not have done in 2006, and definitely didn't do after Terry let Nash tie that final game in 2005. "Forget it," you told him. "I've got your back."

"I think in this league, you have to play until the end," you said after. You finished with twenty-four points (on ten of twenty-two shooting) and eleven rebounds. "We kept believing, kept playing off each other."

Charles Barkley, now the Mavs' biggest evangelist, said on NBATV, "They talk about champagne and Mercedes-Benz, but Dirk Nowitzki is the greatest European import ever."

⊕   ⊕   ⊕

Unlike 2006, I actually went to the trouble of getting a media credential for the Finals. I had to go down to the AAC a day or two before and get my photo taken in a trailer the NBA had set up in a parking lot. The pass got me in the building, but it didn't get me a seat. I hadn't thought about where I would watch the game and didn't realize until I arrived that the only place for me was in the media workroom. I also realized that I wasn't there to cover the Finals. How could I? I was really going to sit and there and be professional and not live and die with every possession? With every shot you took? I wasn't going to clap and scream and boo and talk shit and curse? I wasn't going to yell, *I see you, Big German*, until my voice sounded like a pile of asphalt had been granted sentience?

I showed up, walked out of the tunnel and onto the court before Game 3 and looked around, really taking in the whole scene—the blue shirts draped over chairs, the Finals logo on the court—and

immediately left. I went to a bar called the Windmill Lounge, a dive a few miles away, getting there a little bit after tipoff. It was better to watch the game as a fan, to watch all of them as a fan, at a bar or at home, or someone's house, rather than trying to be in the building but having to try to be impartial.

Even if they lost—and I suppose *especially* if they lost—I would have rather experienced that as a fan and not have to worry about keeping my composure.

"We're going to approach the next one like it's our last," you'd said between Games 2 and 3. "You cannot get a split and a huge emotional win in Game 2 and then go home and lose Game 3."

You lost Game 3, 88–86.

Chris Bosh, graduate of Dallas' Lincoln High School, hit the game winner from sixteen feet with 39.6 seconds left, after you had tied the score at 86 with a personal 10-0 run. You had a chance to tie it again at the buzzer, but you couldn't get the shot to fall.

"The look was as good as you get," you said. You'd done everything you could. You had thirty-four points, fifteen in the fourth alone, going 11–21 with what the *Wall Street Journal* called, in a headline, "a shot so ugly you can't stop it."

But maybe that wouldn't be enough.

Maybe you this would continue to mirror 2006, taking a slightly different path to the same result.

Maybe the Heat were just too good, better than they had been back then, now with James and Bosh.

Maybe it just wasn't meant to be. Not everyone gets to win a championship.

Maybe

Maybe

Maybe

Maybe

Maybe

Maybe

Maybe

M
a
y
b

e

Or maybe not.

Game 4 was your version of Michael Jordan's Flu Game. The night before, you'd come down with a sinus infection. You showed up to shootaround looking like "a ghost," as Donnie Nelson put it. I understand; I get one every eighteen months. It feels like someone has opened a tiny black hole one inch behind your cheekbones. "Every time he started to talk, he started coughing," Chandler said. "He was wheezing."

You were sent to the locker room and then home, loaded up with medicine. But everyone could see that you hadn't improved much when you came back for the game. "Dirk is a playful guy and outgoing and outspoken when it comes to the locker room," Chandler said. "Seeing him not being playful and not really saying much and kind of sitting in his locker, I knew it was going to be a tough night for him."

While the team tried to keep your illness a secret, it was obvious something was wrong. Battling a 101-degree fever, you missed ten of eleven shots at one point, and missed a free throw, breaking your second streak of thirty-nine straight in that playoff run. But you stuck it out. You stayed in your chair as long as possible during timeouts, getting every second of rest that you could, only going back on the court when you absolutely had to. You pulled down eleven rebounds and scored ten of your twenty-one points in the fourth, as the Mavs outscored the Heat 21–9 over the last ten minutes of the game to win 86–83. And you refused to see any of it as being out of the ordinary. "After playing eight, nine months on a high level, nobody is completely healthy. It's time to fight through some stuff."

Donnie Nelson said it was "our version of Willis Reed," recalling when the Knicks center limped out to start Game 7 against the Lakers in the 1970 Finals, playing on a torn muscle in his thigh. "I think last night was one of the most inspirational, gut performances in Mavs history," he said. "If he doesn't tough it out and if he doesn't come back, there is no way. I don't even know how he was standing in that fourth quarter, because that was a physically taxing game. We're here at 2–2 because of him."

You went home, took a shower, slurped chicken soup and hot tea, and slept, finally. When you woke up, you were ready to go again, or ready enough. You still didn't change your routine much. You went to the gym in the afternoon to get some shots up and get a sweat going. You lived for that time. "Basically, for a month and a half, two months, you're living on the edge every night. You're thinking about it—eat, breathe, sleep basketball—and that's what's fun about the playoffs, but also very draining."

It would be a race, then, to see if you could win before your body gave up on the 2010–11 season. "We have one more week to go, both teams, and we're going to go for it. Both teams are going to get their vacation afterward." By shootaround on Thursday morning, the day of Game 5, you were as close to 100 percent as you could get, or at least putting on a good show for everyone. You needed to. "This is our Game 7 here," you said, because you couldn't give Miami two chances to close out the series at home.

You said then and I'm sure you would say now that what

happened next didn't have any effect on you. And maybe it was only us, your fans, your protectors, that took it personally. And maybe that's how it always was and had been, and why should it be any different then? Maybe you needed to be stoic and let us handle the emotions. Maybe we needed that division of labor, too.

But maybe you cared more than you let on.

"The intensity Dirk had after having his illness questioned by D-Wade and LeBron, I think it's understated how being in that situation drove him in that moment," Casey Smith said when I asked him about it later. "At least in my opinion."

A day after Game 4, Wade was already waving away any sort of Flu Game talking points: "Everyone is injured at this time," he said. "I'm not going to get into the fun-loving story of him being sick. Once you show up on the court, you show up on the court. Everyone is equal. He's a great player without all the dramatics of the stories that's been going on."

Wade had a point, probably, and probably it would have been more effective not coming from a player who once had an entire ad campaign for Converse built around the tagline, "Fall seven times. Stand up eight," with video going all the way back to his high school days of him determinedly rising after taking a spill on the court. But, whatever, OK. Remember what happened next?

After the Heat's shootaround before Game 5, while walking back to the locker room with James, Wade coughed and turned to his teammate. "Whoa, did y'all hear me cough? Think I'm getting

sick." James coughed into his shirt and giggled. CBS 11 in Dallas caught it on camera, and Wade later confusingly said that he knew people would make too much of his joke, which is why he did it. I . . . guess?

As far as motivation goes, you didn't hear about the video or the jokes or any of it until Friday. By then, the Mavs had won Game 5 behind your twenty-nine points, which included a go-ahead dunk with 2:45 left. James had a triple-double, but the Mavs still closed out the 112–103 victory on a 17–4 run. Fans at the AAC were wearing blue giveaway shirts with THE TIME IS NOW on the front. It was feeling that way.

When you were told about the video, you said Wade and James were "a little childish, a little ignorant."

"I've been in the league thirteen years. I've never faked an injury before," you said. But you tried to quash it. "It's not going to add anything extra to me. This is the NBA Finals. If you need extra motivation, you have a problem."

You were right, of course, but it was frustrating. You weren't even allowed to be tough when you were being tough. I couldn't help but be angry on your behalf.

But it made sense. After coming to your defense all these years, we needed our moment in the Finals, too.

You were one win away.

⊕ ⊕ ⊕

"No matter where you see Dirk in the whole scheme of things, he's put this team on his back," Donnie said before Game 6 in Miami, "the first time the true alpha dog has been European."

And then, after seventy-three games in the regular season and twenty more in the playoffs, you suddenly you weren't. You'd pushed the stone uphill for four years, and now that the top of the mountain was in sight, it started to slip. You missed eleven of your first twelve shots—a wide-open three in the corner, pull-ups, one-legged fade-aways that would normally get rung up on the scoreboard before they even reached the rim.

I don't know what it's like to play in an NBA game, much less the deciding game of a championship series, and I can barely recollect my days as a competitive basketball player. But I know what it's like to want something so much that you start fucking up when it's close, right there, practically yours but agonizingly not quite yet. How the more you want and try and push the worse it gets, a fire that your desperation is only fueling, like you're sweating gasoline. I do know that. I've been one for twelve in life plenty of times. If I'm being honest, I am right now. I know what you were feeling.

Brian Cardinal knew what you needed. "At halftime, we're all trying to figure it out," Cardinal told me. "He's trying to figure out how to play a little better. We're all trying to figure out how we can win this game and win the championship. I still remember going in the locker room and trying to pump everybody up and give them fives and talking to them, saying, 'This is right where we

want them.' And I still remember going up to Dirk and saying in front of folks, 'Hey, I love it. I love it. You've got them right where you want them. You got all your misses out of the way. There's no way you're going to shoot that bad in the second half.' Just trying to gas up the situation. He looks at me, he's like, 'Dude, you're nuts.'

"And he came out and played better. Honestly, I have no idea if what I said helped impact anything, but my goal was just to have him relax. Have him calm down a bit. Have him take a breath. So, hopefully, for one split second, he's thinking about me being a knucklehead and not worrying about the game."

You made your first shot of the second half, twelve seconds in, a seventeen-footer on an assist from Kidd. The Heat took the lead a couple of minutes later, held it for sixteen seconds, and never got closer than seven in the fourth quarter. You shot eight of fifteen in the second half, finishing with twenty-one points and eleven rebounds in a 105–95 win. You didn't back into a championship. You didn't make your teammates carry you over the line. You grabbed control of the game in the third and fourth quarters. Like Chandler said, they just had to get you there. For the series, you had sixty-two fourth-quarter points; James had eighteen. You shot 18–35 from the field in the final periods—including 5–8 in Game 6, with Terry telling you "Remember '06" throughout—and a perfect 24–24 from the foul line.

Almost everyone had a moment in Game 6. Terry had twenty-seven points (on brilliant 11–16 shooting). Marion had twelve points and eight rebounds and his usual great defense. Kidd had

eight assists. J.J. Barea had fifteen points and DeShawn Stevenson had three big first-half threes.[40] Reserve center Ian Mahinmi hit a rare jumper to beat the third-quarter buzzer (and a surprisingly deft one-legged fadeaway earlier). And Cardinal, in addition to his halftime antics, nailed a three and drew an offensive foul on Wade. *We just got to get this man there.*

Here's what I remember on the screen at Joe's house: with 18.8 seconds left and Kidd shooting free throws, you and Terry hugged at midcourt, then you walked to the other foul line and let out a long breath. *Hell yes.* You would turn thirty-three in exactly one week. I would turn thirty-seven the next day.

Mario Chalmers hit a three with sixteen seconds left to end the scoring, and while the Mavs dribbled out the clock, you left the court. You hopped over the scorer's table and went to the locker room, overcome by the moment and unwilling to share it or exploit it. You lay down on the floor and cried. I've always wondered what those few minutes in the locker room were like. I've had the chance to ask you, but the truth is, I don't want to know the specifics, not beyond what I already know. That moment belongs to you. You have already given me, given us, given Dallas enough. You never stopped believing in us.

Before the 2010–2011 season, when you were a free agent, I began to steel myself for the idea of seeing you in another uniform or, worse, not seeing you on the court at all. It seemed like it was getting to be almost that time. You had been in the league for a dozen

---

40. And sank thirteen of twenty-three from behind the arc for the series.

years by then, and sports franchises in Dallas weren't any more loyal than those in other cities. Emmitt Smith took his final handoffs in Arizona. Tony Romo was nudged toward the broadcast booth when he probably had a few more passes left in him. The last time Mike Modano took the ice, it was in a Detroit Red Wings sweater. None of the great Dallas Mavericks that came before you finished their careers with the team. We had to watch Michael Finley win a title with the Spurs, in 2007.

You could have left, and no one could have held it against you if you had, if you had taken your talents to Phoenix to rejoin your buddy Steve Nash for one more run, or to L.A. to pair with Kobe Bryant, coming off back-to-back titles, or somewhere else. (As long as it wasn't Golden State or Miami—it was still too soon. OK, or San Antonio, either.) But you stayed in Dallas, and, more than that, you became a real Dallasite, enmeshing yourself in the city and its culture.

It would have, obviously, been incredible to win a championship in 2006 or 2007. But this was somehow better, because you didn't give up on us. The least we can give you, the least I can give you, is that moment by yourself in the locker room.

Eventually, your buddy Scott Tomlin, a PR guy for the team, coaxed you back out to the floor to celebrate with your teammates. Don Carter, the cowboy who started the franchise, got the Larry O'Brien Trophy first. Then Cuban. Then you. Then Celtics legend Bill Russell presented you with the Finals MVP trophy.

"Nowitzki is one of the greatest players in the history of the game, and that has been validated here tonight," Carlisle said. Erik

Spoelstra called you "indefensible." "His game has continued to elevate in his thirties," the Heat coach said. "That's a remarkable thing."

Back in Würzburg, where hundreds gathered to watch, your dad said, "It really is something special for Dirk because he's finally recognized in America, too, as a real sporting great."

It was one of the best playoff runs ever: you beat Kobe Bryant and Pau Gasol, Kevin Durant, Russell Westbrook, and James Harden, Brandon Roy and LaMarcus Aldridge, and LeBron James, Dwyane Wade, and Chris Bosh, all in the same postseason. You had six games scoring thirty-plus points, finishing with averages of 27.7 points, 8.1 rebounds, 2.5 assists, and shooting percentages of 49 percent from the field, 46 percent from three, and 94 percent from the free-throw line. No one had ever done that before, and no one has done it since.[41] You didn't have an easy road. It didn't align perfectly. You went through the defending champions and their presumptive successors. And it wasn't a fluke or an accident.

Where did you rank after? Does it matter? Someone said after Game 6 that you "carried [your] team like no other MVP since Jordan" and it sounds wild, but it is also undeniable.

"I still can't believe it," you said. "This team has ridden a lot of ups and downs, always stayed together.

"Still can't believe it."

---

41. OK, technically, Hakeem Olajuwon also shot over 46 percent on three-pointers: he made two of four in twenty-three games; you made twenty-four of fifty in twenty-one games.

⊕ ⊕ ⊕

I have a photo on my phone, and it's been on three or four phones now, and it'll be on three or four more. Whenever I run across it while looking for something else, I post it on Instagram or Facebook or text it to Isaac, or all three. Just before I wrote these sentences, I sent it to Isaac three feet away on the couch across from me. Mostly, I just look at it and remember.

It's not technically a good photo, no offense to my friend Jessica, who took it without me knowing and sent it to me a few days later. It's blurry, a bit blown out, a stray arm is jutting into the frame. But none of that matters. It's perfect as is.

Jessica took it a few seconds after Game 6 ended. Isaac, as I said before, had started taking off his shirt when he got excited, like changing into a superhero costume in reverse. He had to release his energy into the universe, and, to do so, he had to be topless. During this game, after he'd removed his shirt, he became so overcome that he bounced into the stand holding Joe's TV and almost brought the seventy-inch screen on top of him. He calmed down after that, a little bit. But the shirt stayed off, and so in the photo, Isaac is tiny and shirtless and jumping into my arms, his left arm wrapping around my neck, his right fist almost punching the ceiling. My eyes are closed tight, and my arms are around him even tighter, and I look like I'm about to crush his little torso, and I can't believe he was ever so small or we were both so happy. It's pure joy, for the Mavs and for each other.

We left not long after and drove home the long way, through Oak Cliff and through downtown, the streets choked with cars honking at each other and at nothing, not one of them unhappily.

⊕   ⊕   ⊕

I have another photo taken in the wake of the championship that I see even more often than the one of me and Isaac that is on my phone, because this one is on my refrigerator.

At some point during the Finals, my editor at *D Magazine*, Tim Rogers, had brought up the idea of putting you on the cover if the Mavs won the title, and just the suggestion, not spoken but sent in a text, made me feel like we were outlining a parade route, tempting the basketball gods to kick the ladder out from under us again.

But even though it was almost enough to chest-pass a black cat in your path, we didn't jinx you, and somehow in the aftermath of Game 6 we arranged for our photographer, Marc Montoya, and his producer wife, Kristen, to set up on the court at the AAC a couple of days later when the team made it back to Dallas and met with the assembled media. The Mavs PR folks said they'd bring you to us— Tim and I showed up, because there was no way we were missing this—and we'd get ten minutes.

After a bit of a delay—there were *a lot* of people waiting for you—you came strolling out across the court to the Montoyas' portable backdrop, looking like a college sophomore in slides, white basketball shorts, and a red Nike JUST DUNK IT T-shirt.

Marc was so excited that he didn't even need the full ten minutes, getting from the first frame to the last in around seven. After Marc got his shot—and you know what ended up on the cover because it's still all over town, a close-up of you with your eyes closed dreamily and a beatific smile, the kind of peace you only see faked in Corona commercials and yoga studio Instagram Stories; it's the smile of someone who has let go of the past and doesn't have to deal with the future yet, perfectly at ease in the present—after that, you agreed to take a photo with me and Tim.

We had photographed you for the magazine once before, a couple of years earlier, for an oral history I had put together for your first decade in Dallas. You agreed to wear a throwback uniform we had specially made for you, even after it showed up half an hour late, and you even rolled up the waistband of the shorts to make them extra short, and you didn't complain when our photographer almost knocked her light rig over on top of you. And after all of *that*, we put a photo of Kurobuta pork jowls on the cover instead of you. (In our defense, it was our annual Best Restaurants issue.)

When Tim and I got on either side of you for our photo, you asked if you were going to be on the cover this time—or were we going with the pork jowls again.

I think about that little joke every time I see that photo, so I think about that joke almost every day.

⊕ ⊕ ⊕

I guess, in retrospect, no one should be surprised that it finally happened for you in 2011. You were in love.

I know that love is not without its own complications and I also know that love makes everything else less complicated. I don't know exactly why, but to me, it's like your life gets an alpha dog and the rest falls in line behind it. Basically, love is you, and everything else becomes the other 2010–11 Dallas Mavericks, serving a purpose, playing a part, following the leader. I know that sounds stupid. But love can make you sound like that, too.

You met Jessica Olsson in February 2010, the weekend the NBA All-Star Game festivities were in Dallas. You were at a charity event for the Sports for Education and Economic Development (SEED) Project, and so was she. She was a transplant like you, born to a Kenyan mother and Swedish father, in Dallas working for the Goss-Michael Foundation art gallery at the time, and she was part of SEED's host committee. Like you, she was raised in an athletic family. Her younger twin brothers, Marcus and Martin, both play professional soccer in England. Her game is tennis.

"I went there and I know her boss and started talking a bit," you told me. "The rest is history."

The two of you had only been seen around Dallas here and there, not really enough to establish you as a couple, your relationship not exactly secret but certainly private. It snuck out a bit just before the Finals, when rumors of an engagement spread. But the first real confirmation that you were together was exactly right, a

month after Game 6, when you walked the red carpet at the ESPY Awards at L.A. Live's Nokia Theatre. You were to be named Best NBA Player and Best Male Athlete. In front of the cameras, you and Jessica kissed. Evan Turner, then with the 76ers, tweeted, "Well I'll be damned. Dirk got him a sister."

It wasn't the end of your victory lap. It was the beginning, of that and so much more. The first half of your career was spent living and dying for a championship (and, not intentionally, the personal glory that accompanied such things). The second half—not perfectly divided, but there is a definite before and after point—would be spent proving that maybe those things don't matter, even if you never completely came around to that viewpoint. The first half would have been most players' *entire* careers, both in length (thirteen seasons) and focus, not to mention achievement. You at least, in the years after 2011, softened your stance from winning a championship being the "only thing" to "most important thing" and maybe even "most important thing in my career but possibly not even top five in my life." Given where you were as late as January 2010, that was a massive change.

"He was a guy that didn't really have hobbies," your friend Brian Dameris told me. "Literally didn't enjoy anything but watching hoops and practice."

But then you had Jessica—you were married in July 2012, with ceremonies in Germany and Kenya—and soon you had a family, too.

⊕   ⊕   ⊕

Over thirteen seasons, you became Dallas and Dallas became you and I was wrapped up in there somewhere, identifying with one or the other or both. Dallas has an inferiority complex still, but at that time maybe you did, too, and at this time maybe I do, too.

You represented us broadly and specifically, able to stand in for the city and for the people in it, coming close to the top so many times only to chutes-and-ladders back to the bottom. I wanted you to beat Miami for yourself, but also for Dallas and also for me. We needed a win. I needed a win.

It's not even that, or just that. Maybe I'm alone here, maybe I'm generalizing, but sometimes, a lot of times, I don't even need a win. I just don't want a loss. I just want to Ctrl-F "Dallas" in the latest dumb news story of the day and get zero hits. I just don't want us to embarrass ourselves. And I actually don't think I'm alone and I don't think I'm generalizing.

When 2011 happened, it wasn't that it was unexpected. It was that it was an occurrence that people had stopped applying expectations to by then. The idea of winning a championship was like a dog that had wandered away from our campsite three or four years ago and then miraculously showed up on our doorstep. It was something we hoped would happen but had given up expecting.

At the outset of the playoffs, in April, I had the same goofy hope I'd had since 2003—that we had you, so we had a chance. *Maybe this will be the year.* You could have stepped in an actual bear trap before a game and I would have argued that your game wasn't built on speed or athleticism, so you would probably be OK. But I don't

know if I still believed it and I don't know when I stopped. Maybe the year before, when you guys went into the postseason as the No. 2 seed and lost to the Spurs again and it just seemed like nothing would ever change.

And then you did it. You fucking did it.

The Big German
Enters the Dark Forest
of Not Quite

Your reward for finally winning a championship was a lockout.

It lasted from July 1 until December 8 and pushed back the start of the 2011–12 season until Christmas Day, almost two months late. But there was an odd symmetry to it. The beginning of your NBA career had been delayed by the previous work stoppage, from July 1998 until January 1999, and now, after you reached the pinnacle of the sport, your defense of the Mavs' first title would be delayed by another one. A parenthesis had been closed.

When the team showed up after the lockout concluded, it was changed to the point of being unrecognizable. One could argue that the Mavs never actually defended the 2011 title, since so many key contributors were gone, largely because Cuban was worried about the salary implications resulting from the renegotiated collective bargaining agreement. Peja Stojaković was gone and so was the man he had replaced, Caron Butler. Playoff heroes DeShawn Stevenson and J.J. Barea were gone. Corey Brewer, gone. The most difficult departure to take was that of Tyson Chandler, off to the Knicks, where he would win Defensive Player of the Year and help propel the team to

fifty wins. They were replaced by Vince Carter (who was great), Yi Jianlian and Brandan Wright (who were definitely on the team), and Lamar Odom (who never really was).

It was a short, odd season, one in which the Mavs simultaneously seemed to be better and worse than they were. The team entered the playoffs as the No. 8 seed, but it still had you and you were still at the top of your game. This was not a normal 1 vs. 8 matchup. But it turned into one anyway.

"We got swept by the Thunder, who happened to go to the Finals that year, but we actually almost should have stole [*sic*] both games in OKC," you told me later. You made two free throws to give the Mavs the lead in Game 1 with just nine seconds left, only to see Kevin Durant win it with a fifteen-foot jumper just before the buzzer. Game 2, the Mavs lost by three, despite your thirty-one points (including 11–11 from the free-throw line). "We were thinking, 'Man, we got 'em right there.' And then we came home and lose and have no shot, basically, in Game 3 and Game 4." The Thunder won the first game in Dallas by sixteen and the next going away, outscoring the Mavs by nineteen in the fourth.

Your reign as champion was officially over.

⊕   ⊕   ⊕

Isaac started playing basketball a couple of years before you won the championship—first with a team delightfully named the Blue Star Wars—but he took it much more seriously after. So seriously that

he was ejected from a game in January 2012. This wasn't your fault.

It was early in the fourth quarter and a player from the other team broke free for what looked to be, even for an eight-year-old, an easy layup. Isaac caught up to him near the basket and brought his arm down over both the kid's wrists before he could get the ball up. He may have grabbed one of the player's arms, too, I'm not sure, but it was a standard-issue hard foul. *No easy baskets.* It was a smart play for a high school game and maybe even junior high, but probably not for a seven-year-old playing against seven- and eight-year-olds, and so they tossed him. He was so frustrated and upset—with himself and the game—that he disappeared afterward for what felt like an hour but was probably more like five minutes. I found him crying behind a stack of tumbling mats.

I made sure he was OK, but I didn't have to ask where he learned a play like that, because I already knew: the 1988–1990 "Bad Boys" Detroit Pistons. His obsession with basketball was kindled by Magic and Bird, then grew into a fire during the championship run, and then it spread across the entire history of the sport. Isaac had been drawn to finesse and flash, but for some reason Motor City resonated with him.

Since Isaac began playing, I helped coach his teams, first as an assistant (with the Blue Star Wars) and then head coach (with the less awesomely named Wildcats and Falcons). The most exasperating part of the gig—and obviously my expectations were out of line with reality and I very well know that—is that, especially when they are starting out, kids do not like to pass the ball. They just want to dribble some

and shoot from anywhere they happen to be. They want to be you. Or they used to. Now they want to be Steph Curry or Trae Young or Luka Dončić. But you know what I mean. As a coach, you want the kids to learn and to have fun, but you also can't help but want *basketball* and you just have to sort of make peace with the fact that they are going to get out on the court and run around and throw the ball in the general direction of the basket, and this goes on for years.

Do you think Holger could have picked you out of that swarm of bees?

Isaac was just like the rest of them, at first. But as you and the Mavs were heading toward your destiny, he began to change. He was already on a basketball team, but now he was becoming a real basketball player. He could understand and appreciate the two-man game you worked with Jason Terry. And once I could see he was grasping larger concepts, I pounced. One weekend afternoon, after shooting around in our driveway for a bit, I showed him a couple of highlight videos of 1970s legend "Pistol" Pete Maravich on YouTube. I wanted Isaac to see that passing could be every bit as exciting as shooting and scoring. He'd had a glimmer of that when we watched the sick-day documentary about Magic and Bird, but this was another level. I've always been drawn to Maravich's style, passes that were generally so unnecessary, less about deceiving his opponents and more about proving that he could deceive his opponents. It was like the difference between a great pool player and a hustler. I thought Isaac might respect that, too.

It worked. He was mesmerized by the blank-faced magician he

saw in those clips, the lanky guy playing in 6/8 time in a 4/4 game. We went back outside, and he started trying to throw no-look passes, flipping the ball over his shoulder and around his back and through his legs, which were barely long enough to slip a ball through. It was a chaos of ideas without any clue as to how to actually execute any of them. Almost none of it worked on purpose, but he was hooked all the same. I had no idea how much. By the time I saw him again the next week, he'd exhausted YouTube's supply of Pistol Pete videos. I think he even watched the clips that had been uploaded from Maravich's *Homework Basketball* series of instructional tapes, featuring a haggard, mustachioed Pete circa the late 1980s, still casually pulling off the ridiculous in a polo shirt and blue sweatpants. Isaac had made his mother rent (and watch with him) *The Pistol: The Birth of a Legend*. He'd read everything that he could find, and I still don't know exactly how he found what he could.

It spiraled out from there. He extended his research to other players, happy enough watching you and the Mavs but also endlessly fascinated by what came before. I didn't mind this at all. I didn't force anything on him—not after those first few YouTube clips—but I definitely encouraged and absolutely enabled him. And I never forgot how lucky I was that we had found our thing. Our first thing, at least, but that's always the most important.

The Mavs' championship run had located this island for us, this safe spot to retreat to when everything else was fraught, a frayed nerve, when we had to push pause on the world. Now we were making it into a second home.

I could barely keep up with him. More or less as a way to occupy him, I bought Isaac a copy of *SLAM* magazine's special issue devoted to the five hundred greatest NBA players of all time. Even though it was published in 2011, and I think determined well before you won your title, you came in at No. 55,[42] a spot ahead of Connie Hawkins and just behind Reggie Miller, an injustice Isaac and I discussed often and in great detail. He practically memorized the entire list, from Michael Jordan to Pervis Ellison. Eventually, the issue fell apart, its pages wrinkled and crinkled and worn and torn like a treasure map, which it pretty much was, except instead of a wooden chest full of doubloons it led to more YouTube searches and odd questions like, "Was Bob Pettit a good dunker?" (No, but I'm pretty sure he was a racist.) He learned how to mimic Elgin Baylor's hanging jumper and, on his own bedroom-door basketball hoop, the way James Worthy finished fast breaks. Just before he was ejected from that youth basketball game, that copy of *SLAM* had led him to a brief infatuation with Isaiah Thomas and those Pistons teams.

But Maravich remained an obsession, which led to him going as the Pistol for Halloween around that time. His mom found a blank jersey in Atlanta Hawks colors and finished it off with iron-ons: Hawks on the front, "Pistol" on the back, No. 44 on both sides. He wore a matching pair of girls' running shorts, because those were the only ones 1970s-short enough. He personalized a pair of white Chuck Taylors himself. With his floppy hair, he made a pretty

42. Your buddy Steve Nash was No. 50.

convincing Pistol Pete, not that any of his friends knew who that was. Nor did any of their parents, for that matter.

I always knew I was lucky.

⊕ ⊕ ⊕

The 2012–13 season was the first time you missed the playoffs since 2001, when you were twenty-one. Jason Terry was gone, signing with Boston before the season, and the only players remaining from the championship roster were Shawn Marion, Roddy Beaubois, Dominique Jones, and you. Chris Kaman, Jae Crowder, Elton Brand, and O.J. Mayo had joined a team that would finish 41–41. It was a weird squad. But it is my favorite postchampionship version of you and it's one of my favorite seasons of yours with no qualifier necessary.

This was when you and some of your teammates stopped shaving during the second half of the season, as the team struggled to make it back to a .500 record, an uphill climb that it was partly at the bottom of because you missed the first twenty-seven games. You'd had to have your right knee drained of fluid twice in the preseason to reduce swelling and finally opted for surgery. It was incredible that your body had held up so well for so long. Prior to that point, over the previous fourteen seasons, you had missed a total of forty-five games, which is pretty unbelievable given the amount of times I remember you leaving the court after stepping on Bruce Bowen's foot, which was like a land mine in a sneaker.

After you came back for your first appearance of the 2012–13 campaign, playing twenty minutes in a thirty-eight-point blowout loss in San Antonio just before Christmas, the Mavs were 12–16 and halfway through a loss that would reach six games. On January 9, after another four-game losing streak, the team was 13–23, ten games below .500, the nadir.

It could have been so much different. It was supposed to have been.

In an alternate universe, a timeline not separated from this one by much, 2012–13 was the first season that Chris Paul and Dwight Howard played together in Dallas, teaming up to make you the most unguardable third option since the invention of the word "maybe." There was no guarantee of championships—in our universe, the Lakers' acquisition of the fart- and fart joke-loving center was like making a green smoothie out of poison ivy, and Paul has infamously never made it to the Finals—but both would have been entering their primes while joining a stable, winning organization led by a singularly selfless, focused superstar in a city with a bit less glare than L.A., where they both ended up.

It really almost happened. I don't want to bring up bad memories, but it did. The Mavs tried to put together trades for both, separately, but did not have enough. Paul was ready to wait until the summer of 2012 to join the Mavs as a free agent, if Howard would commit as well. But Howard, desperately afraid of being unliked because he has the personality of a six-foot-ten middle schooler,

opted into his contract with Orlando, postponing his free agency by another season, and Paul wouldn't wait that long. He was sent to the Clippers in 2011 after requesting a trade.

Instead of assembling a super team, the Mavs assembled a super odd one, the home team for the Island of Misfit Toys. Elton Brand was in his thirteenth season. Vince Carter in his fourteenth (though he would continue playing until 2020). Former Lakers point guard Derek Fisher was around for nine games at the beginning before engineering his way to Oklahoma City, which was fine, because he was hard to root for. Eddy Curry, one of the Baby Bulls drafted in Chicago with Tyson Chandler, played the final two games of his NBA career with us that season. Chris Kaman, your German National Team buddy, was there. Jae Crowder was a rookie. And O.J. Mayo had come over from Memphis and was really good.[43]

Looking back on it, I'm still unsure how you got back to .500.

The season wasn't completely lost by the time you came back from your knee surgery in December, but by then there wasn't much to play for except pride. Which would too often be the case from July 2011 until April 2019.

But pride was more than enough. You guys added another wrinkle, less as motivation and more as a symbol of solidarity. Not long after the season had reached its lowest point—and it had been a long time since a Mavs team had been *that* bad—you, Carter, Kaman,

---

43. Averaging more than fifteen points along with 4.4 assists and 3.5 rebounds, while appearing in all eighty-two games.

Mayo, Crowder, and Dahntay Jones stopped shaving, and agreed not to until a .500 record was reached.

You played in fifty-three of the final fifty-five games, showing some signs of slippage but still capable of brilliance, such as in a late February game against Milwaukee when you pulled down twenty rebounds to go with your twenty-one points. By April—and I know sports isn't life and death—you really looked like a warrior, a giant This! Is! SPARTA! beard springing from your jaw. The team went almost four months between .500 records, from 11–11 in December until finally making it back on April 14, a 107–89 win over New Orleans that put the Mavs at 40–40.

You shaved immediately after, still in uniform, still sweaty.

It was the lowest stakes you'd played for since your early twenties. You weren't DIRK yet then. The door wasn't completely open to the possibilities the Nelsons told us lurked inside, but it was cracked enough where one could see the future, be tantalized by the glimpse. Now, a different door was starting to open, still just ajar but getting wider all the time, and now it was possible to see what the rest of your career would look like, and what you—even in slight decline—would mean to Dallas and the Mavs and me and everyone else.

⊕   ⊕   ⊕

Even as the championship in 2011 got further away, there were still people who wanted more from you. It wasn't your fault, but you had conditioned fans to expect the impossible, demand the unlikely. And

you still looked like the player who had led the team on that magical run, and still played like it most of the time, even as you hit your midthirties. In 2013–14, you were an All-Star (again)—not at your peak, but not far off,[44] still capable of turning a half of basketball into a game of HORSE, with those wrong-foot fadeaway jumpers delivered from barely plausible angles, like someone who had never watched a second of basketball had stuck one of those Fathead vinyl stickers of you on a wall in the dark. You should have been a sidekick at that point in your NBA life, maybe coming off the bench, but you were still the Mavs' focal point, the sun that Monta Ellis and Vince Carter and everyone else orbited.

And yet. I remember going to the Mavs' first preseason game, against New Orleans, and hearing someone *heckling* you. "Oh, come on, Dirk!" this guy said after you missed a shot or let your man score or something, which wouldn't have been the worst thing in the world in a playoff game, given everything you'd already done, but was especially insignificant in the first quarter of the first preseason game.

That's the one I remember the most, but it happened all the time. People pretend like your transition to infallible franchise icon was seamless, that the championship granted you a lifetime free pass from the fanbase the instant the clock expired in Miami in Game 6. But that's not quite true. *Oh, come on, Dirk!* Did you hear it, too? Every minor or even perceived miscue turned some fans into

---

44. You were within rounding distance of another 50-40-90 shooting season and averaged 21.7 points, 6.2 rebounds, and 2.7 assists.

impatient youth basketball coaches, the kind you'd never want your kids to play for, the kind I always did my very best not to be.

I think part of it is that Dallas sees itself as a city of winners, even when that is shown not to be true, and though you had at last proven that you were one, it caught people by surprise. The triumph in 2011 came years after they had written you off, assumed you wouldn't ever get there. When you did, maybe they weren't sure what to do with you. Dallas is still a football town, after all, and to the city's sports fans, you had been slotted as a Danny White or a Tony Romo, not a Roger Staubach or a Troy Aikman. Maybe some of them didn't trust it, or maybe they got greedy. Winners didn't just win once, after all; they won and won and won. Or maybe Dallas simply doesn't know how to handle a win, always wanting more. Think of Klyde Warren Park, a wonderful patch of green built over a highway on the edge of downtown, a masterstroke of planning and foresight decades in the making. Since the park opened in 2012, to universal acclaim, everyone involved has tried to undermine its success by proposing unnecessary features, gaudy upgrades—indoor event space, an ice-skating rink. In November 2020, it was announced that the park would be getting a $10 million "super fountain" that no one asked for or needed. We can't just leave well enough alone.

As for how to handle you, it would take until the next season, and the arrival of Chandler Parsons and then Rajon Rondo, for everyone to get on the same page:

We've had it better than we could have possibly ever hoped and it will never be this good again, at best it will be a different good, and if

we are lucky, if we have somehow done enough to deserve it, this will last for a few more years.

And even if we didn't deserve it, that's exactly what happened. You stayed. You didn't leave us when you could have and honestly maybe should have, after what happened in 2006 and 2007. People generally move out of haunted houses. What those outside of Dallas don't understand is that 1999–2011 didn't make you a legend in the city forever. 2012–2019 did. You could have left, but instead you became even more rooted in Dallas. You could have gone after another championship, but you didn't.

You stayed.

⊕   ⊕   ⊕

For Isaac's tenth birthday, I took him to see the Mavs play the Golden State Warriors. It was 2014 and they weren't quite the juggernaut they would become.[45] Good, but not historically great. Mark Jackson was still coaching them, not Steve Kerr. Steph Curry hadn't been fully weaponized yet, but he was close. It was his breakout season, first time on the All-Star roster, first time on an All-NBA team (he was in the second five). The team would win fifty-one games, just two more than the Mavs.

I'd cashed in a credit I'd had since the 2011 lockout cost me a

---

45. And they were no longer the 2007 Warriors—everyone from that team was finally gone.

bunch of games from the half-season ticket package I had back then, when I could afford it, and we got a pair of seats two rows behind the Warriors bench. If you were a fan of the NBA in general, or the Warriors specifically, it was a great game. I only remember the end, really.

I forgot, until I looked it up, how great you played, scoring eleven points on your own to finish off the last couple of minutes of the first half, ending the night with tenty-two, including six of eight from three, and eleven rebounds. None of it ended up counting for much—not your effort, or mine—because guard Monta Ellis's winning layup attempt was blocked by Jermaine O'Neal, a play that I'm still certain five years later was actually goaltending. And then Curry buried a twenty-one-footer as time expired.

Isaac was actually mad at me for putting him in a position to get punched in the gut like that, like I had been when I was his age and Derek Harper had dribbled out the clock. Like I would be later, again and again and again. I thought it was just the heat of the moment, but he was upset about it for a year or so, only conceding it had been a good birthday present long after, once he understood that was the true experience of being a fan more often than not. The wins sometimes are obscured by the losses, because as good as victory feels, defeat hurts much worse. It only hurts more the better the team is, the higher it ascends, the closer you get.

You'd given Mavs fans the ability to be hurt again, after the numbing ineptitude of almost a full decade at the bottom. You played long enough that you went from having to convince people who had

been burned by the 1990s-era Mavs that basketball paradise was possible here in Dallas, to having to gently let down their offspring, who had been born in it and didn't know anything else existed.

They would find out over the next few years, as the Mavericks went from forty-nine wins to forty-two to thirty-three and twenty-four and thirty-three again, not quite back to the dismal days before you arrived, but not far from. You were stuck on a rebuilding team, trying to find another Dirk Nowitzki. One would arrive in 2018, when Luka Dončić surprisingly fell to the Mavs in the draft, but that meant you spent the twilight of your career losing more than you ever had, roaming the deserts of mediocrity. Even a first-round sweep in the playoffs would have been preferable. It would have been *something*.

But you still had some magic left.

⊕　⊕　⊕

Isaac and I are creatures of habit. I know you understand that. I think you're probably the same. We need constants, buoys floating off the shore of any given week that we can cling to, places where we can call ourselves regulars and order the usual. His mom and I split up just before he turned six, and it hasn't always been easy—an understatement verging on being an outright lie. We've become accustomed to chaos, maybe, probably unfortunately, but we need things we can rely on, and when one disappears, we have to find a replacement.

If you analyze all of our various patterns and routines over the years, at the heart of most of them is basketball, and at the heart of

basketball, for most of his life, was you. A lot of our decisions have been based on: *Where can we watch the game?*

Until recently, we didn't have cable or satellite at home—it's a long story involving a stolen DirecTV box taken in a burglary that I believe was carried out by the guy who used to mow the lawn, who also showed up once near tears when heavy metal icon Ronnie James Dio died—so we were forever in search of some restaurant or somewhat-kid-friendly bar that had a TV (or enough TVs) that would allow us to see the Mavs game. We weren't very particular. Does this make me a divorced-dad stereotype? Perhaps. But stereotypes don't have virgin births. They come from somewhere. We needed a connection, and this is how we made it, and that is where it took us.

All of this is my explanation for how, in 2017, we came to watch you score your 30,000th career point at a scrubby sports bar with a name—Go 4 It Sports Grill—that sounded like it had fallen out of the brain of an eight-year-old kid named Tanner with a permanent fruit-punch goatee. It was a name that sounded like it had been decided on by the designer of generic, non-team-branded sportswear for toddlers, those little sweatshirts that say "Baseball Ace" over a rudimentary illustration of a baseball and a set of fighter-pilot wings for some reason, such an odd combination that it takes you a moment to make the connection because the wordplay, if you could call it that, is actually too obvious, a trick question where the trick is there isn't one.

Anyway, so, yeah: Go 4 It Sports Grill. The staff was nice and the food was food. They had poker tournaments that seemed to double as vaping contests. It was the type of place that always has at least

one guy at the bar who snuck away from home and his wife and kids, saying he was going to the grocery store next door. But that night, as it was many nights, it was a refuge for me and Isaac, because we had each other and we had basketball and we had you.

When everything else was falling apart, had fallen apart, we had those three things. Basketball remains a world we can disappear into together, and at that point, for Isaac's entire life and for as long as I could remember of mine, you were the leader of the escape party, map in hand, ushering us along. And if you think that's giving a sport too much importance, I'd agree, but I'm simply trying to accurately convey what has happened since he was seven and what is happening now and what might happen for the rest of our lives.

So: we were at Go 4 It and you needed to score twenty to cross the 30,000-point threshold. You'd reached twenty only five times that season, and it was then March 7. You had *averaged* twenty points as recently as 2013–14 and just the season before you'd been good for more than eighteen a game. But now there were games in which you didn't even hit double figures, something that was once unthinkable, only possible if you had to leave because of injury or didn't play at all. If your shot was off, you'd make it up by drawing fouls and getting to the free-throw line, and then you'd usually find your rhythm, a few jumpers would fall, and everything would be fine again. If was more difficult for you to get untracked in 2017. If you didn't have it, it wasn't coming.

But twenty points felt doable. The conditions had set up almost perfectly to get it done. It was a home game against the Lakers, so Kobe Bryant would be there, and you usually played better when he was

around. Remember just the year before, when you hit the game-winner on the baseline against them? Kobe was on the bench, in street clothes that night, and your momentum took you right to where he was sitting. He reached out, dapped you up—*I see you, Big German, I see you*—and then you took off back up the court. So you had Kobe. And, two nights earlier, you had had rung up eighteen and put 30,000 within your reach.

You were beyond ready to end the chase so you could go back to normal, to angle the spotlight away from you again, at least until the next milestone. It had been difficult to get Dallas fans to care about anything in that season. The only other highlights had been the emergence of undrafted rookie Yogi Ferrell, who scored thirty-two points in his fourth game with the team after being signed late in the year, and I guess the trade for big man Nerlens Noel, who briefly seemed like the team's center for the future but turned out to barely be its center for the present. The Mavs had faded after a brief run put them close to a playoff spot and would end up winning only thirty-three games.

Conditions had set up almost perfectly for me, too, because the game fell on a Tuesday night, and Tuesday nights Isaac was with me. We got to Go 4 It just before tipoff, just before you gave a forgettable season a reason to exist. It was obvious from the first time you touched the ball that you had cracked open time again. The 2011 version of you was out on the court—the unstoppable, unguardable iteration, mentally and physically peaking, all those sessions with Holger, all the disappointment and desperation that came bundled with it building to this.

You nailed a midrange jumper, then a straight-ahead three, and then you were on a dizzying rush—another three; an and-one jumper following a mean pump fake; a turnaround, of course—and before everyone could catch their breath, you had fourteen points with no misses. The Lakers, as a team, also had fourteen. The electricity came through the screen and deputized Go 4 It, turning it into an overflow section of the American Airlines Center. Burgers were ignored, beers forgotten, everyone in a frenzy, a dormant volcano constructed from old neon beer signs suddenly, violently erupting. Isaac and I looked at each other after every basket, cartoon-wide eyes, jaws no longer functioning, incredulous at what we were seeing.

Thirty thousand points was a huge moment—a plateau only reached at that point by Kareem Abdul-Jabbar, Karl Malone, Kobe Bryant, and Michael Jordan; LeBron James would get there soon— and you were somehow making it bigger, the way only truly great players can, a level only accessible to them. Your first points of your career might have come on a pair of free throws, but you didn't make a habit of backing into these personal triumphs. You got them going away. And that's what you did that night.

Just one minute and two seconds into the second quarter, you sank a baseline jumper over Larry Nance Jr. and got your twenty, which gave you your 30,000, and it was the perfect shot to do it on, like your eventual statue in front of the arena had stepped in for you.

Before play could be halted, you hit another three. Because when you are on, nothing can stop you.

Oh, this old world keeps spinnin' 'round
It's a wonder tall trees ain't laying down
There comes a time

—*Neil Young, "Comes a Time"*

The End

When did you know?

I'm not asking when you knew it was time to tell people, though I was surprised you did it before the season was officially finished. It made more sense when you told me later that "that way, in a month or two, I didn't have to come back and do a big press conference." And *that* made even more sense when, a few months later, you had to basically do that anyway, when the City of Dallas renamed the street in front of the AAC Nowitzki Way. You were appreciative but you also had the posture and body language of a teenager at a dinner party whose parents are bragging about him. It was like the Dirk from 1999 or 2000 had come back to accept the honor.

And I'm not asking when you knew you couldn't do it anymore, because you probably knew that before the season even started, or at least before your season started, a couple of months after everyone else, on December 13 against Phoenix. What I mean by "do it"—be Dirk Nowitzki. You could still play a little bit, and there were flashes of what once was, but rarely full games. You were the old Dirk every once in a while, but mostly you were Old Dirk, sorry. Your stat line in

that Suns game—two points and one rebound in just over five minutes—was not quite the aberration fans would have hoped. It was
more or less the new normal. Even in the game where you passed
Wilt Chamberlain for No. 6 on the NBA's all-time scoring list[46] you
were pretty quiet—eight points in twelve minutes—and you *always*
got up for milestone games, either because it gave you a little extra jolt
of adrenaline or you just wanted it over with as quickly as possible,
or most likely both. Your best game, and one of your few really good
ones, came against the defending-champion Golden State Warriors:
twenty-one points on eight of fourteen shooting, including 5–8 from
three, and five rebounds in a surprise blowout win.

That game happened on March 23, late in the season, and there
was a feeling—or, really, more of a hope—that you were finally ready
to be Dirk Nowitzki again, physically able to be Dirk again, and
maybe you might stick around for one more year, especially since the
team had traded for Kristaps Porzingis, the seven-foot-three Latvian
who had grown up idolizing you.

The next game, three nights later, you had nine points in less
than eleven minutes in a loss to the Sacramento Kings.

"It's just the foot gave me problems all the time, even in good
games," you told me not long after it was over. "At times in the second half, I'd make a shot and I'd come down and it would be shooting in my foot. It just wasn't fun anymore. You know? Unfortunately."

---

46. In a true passing-of-the-torch moment, it came on a fadeaway jumper from
the top of the key on a pass from Luka Dončić.

You could have gotten buckets in a wheelchair. You could have been good for at least one basket until you were fifty, and the Mavs would have let you. Mark Cuban wouldn't have forced you out even if you sat down on the floor on defense and checked your Twitter feed. But even being able to go out there in a limited capacity required exhaustive, almost year-round effort, pre- and post-game treatment, no beer, no sugar, no time off, the game becoming a little less enjoyable every day, life becoming less enjoyable even as you had more of it to enjoy, with Jessica and the kids, the situation nearing untenable.

So I guess what I want to ask is this: When did you know that you didn't *want* to do it anymore? That it was finally just too much?

⊕ ⊕ ⊕

It was not supposed to end like this.

In early April 2018, you underwent a season-ending procedure called a surgical debridement on your left ankle. The team announced that you had been fighting through an ankle impingement all season. In the simplest terms: you had so much scar tissue on your ankle that you couldn't really bend it. In spite of that, you still played seventy-seven games and averaged twelve points on some of the most efficient shooting of your career. Imagine if you could have run, too? That was what the surgery was for. No one was expecting the doctors to turn back the clock. No one was expecting "better than ever"; "better than recently," however, was not out of the question. Being able to move again was certainly a reasonable outcome.

I have to roast you for a second. In your twentieth season, you ran like someone had woken you up from a dead sleep by banging on your door and you were gingerly jogging across the house to see who it was. Ninety percent of the time, it looked like you had *just* stubbed your toe. You ran like a newborn colt with forelegs made of theatrical glass. You moved like you were wearing Nikes with insoles consisting of crushed glass and thumbtacks. It sometimes, maybe a lot of the time, arguably all of the time, seemed like you were playing in a bare feet in a house with two unruly toddlers who loved Legos and hated cleaning them up. It gives me no pleasure to report this, but I am committed to the truth. Your gait was as elegant and graceful as someone saying "surgical debridement" while stifling a yawn.

You were supposed to be ready for training camp, but you had a setback playing in a pickup game, and your ankle never fully healed. (It eventually was healthy enough to play again, but you were still getting treatment on it after you retired.) So, you still couldn't run. If anything, it was worse. You looked like you were wading through a ball pit at a children's pizza restaurant, like your shoes were on the wrong feet, like you'd stepped in dog shit and didn't want to get it on the court. It wasn't easy to watch, especially knowing how hard you had to work just to get to that point.

I wanted to believe otherwise, since you had yet to make a formal announcement. But it was clear: the end wasn't near. It was here.

⊕   ⊕   ⊕

What turned out to be your final home game, against the Phoenix Suns, was styled as a tribute to your twenty-one seasons with the Mavs, an NBA record for longevity with one franchise, and of all the milestones and records in your career, this was the one that seemed to mean the most to the fans and the organization and to you, too. It was proof of a bargain made long ago, of which both sides upheld their ends. You had been there for them, always, and they had been there for you—maybe a little less than always, but close enough.

They called it "41.21.1" and it was a retirement party in all but name. You, of course, brought a gift to your own fete, dropping thirty points—a number you hadn't hit in three years and a total that made you the oldest player, at forty years and 294 days, to score thirty or more, passing Michael Jordan. And as you paid tribute to your own greatness, plenty of others did the same via the arena's video boards. Hall of Famers and legends. Your peers.

Charles Barkley: "Probably my favorite player, because he's just such a great person."

Gregg Popovich: "Dirk is a unique human being, both athletically and as an individual on the planet."

David Robinson: "His consistency, his level of play, is *incredible.*"

LeBron James: "I think what solidifies him as one of the greats, he just continued to get better and better and better and better, to a point where he was unstoppable."

Kevin Durant: "Somebody that was unguardable and created a shot that really can't be blocked."

Allen Iverson: "Big fan, my hero, shot the blood out of that thang."

Hakeem Olajuwon, Kareem Abdul-Jabbar, Nancy Lieberman, Grant Hill, Steve Kerr, Steph Curry, Dikembe Mutombo, Paul George, former teammates Tyson Chandler and Michael Finley, NBA Commissioner Adam Silver, Rick Barry, Kenny Smith, Shaquille O'Neal—they all paid homage with recorded messages.

Could you have imagined that happening the day you met Holger Geschwindner in that gym in Germany?

But it got better. The team had also arranged for some of your idols—Barkley, Scottie Pippen, Detlef Schrempf, Shawn Kemp, and Larry Bird—to surprise you on the court after the game. (Michael Jordan was the only one on your list not in attendance.) A couple of months later, over the phone, you sounded like you still didn't believe it had actually happened. You remained the kid who looked up to those guys, despite everything that had transpired in the decades since. "I didn't think they would make that travel or make that happen for me. You know? I was super shocked."

Seeing them spread out in a semicircle around you was like looking at your basketball DNA under a microscope, examining how the nucleotides fit together. Barkley's play with the 1992 Dream Team had inspired you to wear No. 14. You didn't play like him, necessarily, but you did incorporate his positionless abandon. You had styled your game more after Pippen, the Chicago Bulls star who could shoot, rebound, pass, and handle the ball. Pippen did it all while maintaining a placid, innate Germanness

you wouldn't expect out of someone who had grown up in a tiny town in Arkansas.

Schrempf's contribution was obvious: he was the most famous German basketball player until you arrived in the NBA. But there was a connection on the court, too. He was a prototype: tall enough, at six foot ten, to play in the middle but so skilled that when he came into the league with the Mavs, he played shooting guard.

Kemp, of course, was a hero to every player who came of age in the 1990s, a katana blade slicing through a crowd, a stick of dynamite who could turn a game into *NBA Jam* with one cartoonish, outlandish, gloriously disrespectful dunk after another. And there *was* a trace of that in your early years, the dunks not quite as obscene, to be sure, but the path to get there similar, the quick first step springing from a big-body forward.

Maybe Kemp's presence would have made more sense if the ceremony had happened in 1999 instead of 2019, back when no one except Holger and maybe the Nelsons and probably not even you knew what you could be. You were a Polaroid that had only a few definable shapes inside the blue-green-gray square. You were a text from someone you've been dating for a month, but only the notification on the lock screen—potential, anticipation, hope. You were good and sometimes great, but you were not yet revolutionary, not yet someone who ruined others when they chased after another you or the idea of you. You were not yet a siren song that would lead more than a few general managers to crash on the unforgiving shores of Tall Smooth-Shooting Europe. That would happen a couple of

years later and lead to failures that everyone remembers (Darko Miličić) and others that occupy so few frames (Maciej Lampe) that they are almost subliminal, too ephemeral to remember to forget. Even the Mavs chased it, in players like seven-foot-five Russian Pavel Podkolzin.

And then there was Larry Bird, Larry Legend, the comparison every white player taller than six foot five has had to endure regardless of whether their games and skillsets are at all compatible. But, obviously, you and Larry did have one thing very much in common. You both could "shoot the blood out of that thang."

⊕   ⊕   ⊕

Finally, it was time for you to say goodbye.

You were at center court under dual spotlights, the rest of the arena, the crowd in the lower bowl, all bathed in blue. You lifted the mike but had to wait for the M-V-P! chant to die down before beginning.

You never loved this part.

"Uh, wow—I'm a little overwhelmed, as you would think. Amazing that my heroes came out here for this game. So, thank you guys so much. Love you guys. Grew up watching and idolizing you guys, so this means more than you'll ever know. Mark, can't wait to see what you've got for my jersey retirement. I mean, this is, this is a high bar you set. But."

A pause. *Now.*

"As you guys might expect, this was my last home game." Can you still hear the sounds the crowd made then? Wounded, guttural, 20,000 hopes dashed simultaneously.

"Yeah." You paused again, a long one, twenty full seconds of silence only broken by one extremely wobbly *uhhh*, the syllable unable to support that much weight. You ran your hands through your hair, rubbed your face, breakup body language all over. You tried a joke to help you push through, deflate the importance just a bit. "I'm trying my yoga breathing but it's not really working that well."

But it worked well enough, steadied you. "But this is, obviously, super, super emotional. There's just too many people to thank. Obviously, Mark and Coach and the whole Mavs organization, for not only tonight, for the entire twenty-one years. For all the fans that have supported me. I've put you guys on a hell of a ride, with a lot of ups and downs, and you guys always supported me, so I appreciate it. Of course, my teammates who supported me. I know it's been a rough year for me, physically, but the guys were always great and tried to support me. I've probably had about two hundred teammates in my twenty-one years. They were all great and supported me and pushed me, so I really appreciate them. There's too many to really name, but I'm really appreciative of the guys I played with."

The next part is my favorite. It's a moment of your classic understatement and self-deprecation, a playing-down of your stature that you took to well over the last few years of your career, most memorably when you imitated Vince Carter and Usain Bolt after managing to dunk a lob pass from Steph Curry in the 2015 All-Star Game, a real

dad-in-the-driveway moment. Your personality was always ready for this stage, just waiting for your age to catch up.

"Of course, thank you to the Phoenix Suns for staying out there and letting me have a few buckets tonight. I appreciate it. Even though Jamal stole my show a little bit today," and here you laughed and pointed at Jamal Crawford, the Suns' thirty-nine-year-old reserve guard, who scored fifty-one points off the bench.[47] "I'm a little mad at that." Crawford laughed and covered his head with a towel as the crowd playfully booed.

"No, no. Anyway, so, I want to thank my family. Lot of people flew in from all over the world. Lots from Germany—my dad, my sister, all sorts of people. Anyways, I'm really speechless for that. But Mark, I think you want to say a few words—but it's been an amazing ride and thank you guys for coming out."

You leaned over to hug Cuban and it was over.

⊕   ⊕   ⊕

You hadn't told anyone you were going to announce your retirement that night—Cuban says he only knew when he saw you getting shots in your ankles that morning—and you never said it would be your

---

47. Crawford became the oldest player in league history to top fifty in a game, and it was the fourth franchise that he had scored more than fifty for (along with the Chicago Bulls, Golden State Warriors, and New York Knicks). If no one writes a book about Crawford's career, someone should at least author an epic poem on his behalf.

last season, always demurring, always leaving it at, *Let's finish this one and then we'll see.* And I know that even if you had known all along, you'd never have said a word. You had always avoided the kind of hullaballoo that would come with a farewell tour. I remember back in 2010, before the championship season, when you flew to Dallas to sign a new contract. The team was gathering a big contingent to greet you at the airport, a welcome party to show just how much you meant to the organization, and you found out about the plan and changed your flight.

Yet you still received the attention, whether you wanted it or not, because most people knew. You played long enough that you had two primes—2003–2007 and 2010–2014—and you were still very effective until 2017 and occasionally in 2018. But in 2019, it was plain that time had passed. People recognized that and acted accordingly. There was the February game in Los Angeles against the Clippers, where coach Doc Rivers called a strange timeout with only nine seconds left in the game and his team up nine. He took the mike from the Staples Center's P.A. announcer. Remember?

"One of the greatest of all time," Rivers said, jabbing his finger toward the court where you were, as the crowd got to its feet. "Dirk Nowitzki."

You took in the standing ovation, gave in to the moment, genuinely touched by the gesture, then took your mouthguard out of your sock and got ready to play out the last gasp of your 1,500th career game.

There were bigger gestures, too, like the NBA creating special

roster spots in the All-Star Game for you and your former nemesis Dwyane Wade, who had already said it would be his final year. As the season wound down, it more or less turned into the victory lap you had tried to escape, crowds around the league chanting "We want Dirk!" like you were some freshman walk-on. It was very nice but also a little embarrassing, and I could see why you hadn't wanted any party of a formal farewell tour, with a hashtag and pre- and post-game ceremonies, with keys to cities and commemorative ha-ha rocking chairs and spotlights and everything else.

Anyone who had paid attention to your career couldn't have been surprised that this is how it would end. I should have known. I should have been there, or I should have at least been with Isaac, as I had been for every one of your big moments since 2011.

But when you were out there on the court at the AAC, surrounded by your basketball heroes, saying goodbye, I was on a plane somewhere over the Atlantic Ocean, on my way to Italy by way of Frankfurt, Germany. As it happens, I was flying toward the airport where your long journey began, when you left Würzburg for a three-day visit to Dallas that turned into a lifetime.

I'm trying to make it sound like it was some carefully constructed plan, that I had timed me and my girlfriend's trip to Italy, where she is from, so that I would miss your last two games. That I was on some journey to your origin as you neared the end. I definitely did not do this, at least consciously. I don't want to give my subconscious too much credit, either. That we had a layover in Frankfurt helps the narrative. But it wasn't intentional. One thing is very much true:

I did not want to see it.

I would have been happy for you to remain on the Mavs bench forever, even if you only played a minute, even if you never played at all. Just so there was always the hope that you could, the chance that you might. Even when your body had begun to betray you, you were capable of a play or two that made everyone forget, a sequence that cracked open time and let a twenty-four-year-old version of you back into our world for a brief run.

You'd catch the ball at the end of a delayed break, trailing the play, sliding into the frame unexpectedly, and then you'd bend deep at the knees and let loose a jumper that took its aesthetic from another sport, a lazy flyball, the arc unmistakable, its home inevitable, target unavoidable, not so much being flung at the basket as being returned there, guided back to where it belonged, and then you'd run [*broad wink to the camera*] back up the court, with that familiar sneer-smile, looking like a cop verifying that the powder he'd found in the suspect's apartment was, in fact, cocaine, and then a low fist pump hitting like an uppercut, forever something off in your celebrations just like everything else in your game, an odd angle of approach, a side-step when a defender expected advance or retreat, an inexact connection—and yet never wrong, a plan not a mistake, an adaptation to a problem that few could see and even fewer could recognize as a problem.

You have—*had*—one of the purest jump shots in the history of the NBA, textbook, a Wikihow page demonstrating the best way to shoot a basketball in four steps. But your route to get there was

sometimes a disaster, like a viral video of a panda rolling down a hill and ending up perfectly positioned at the bottom somehow then grabbing a piece of bamboo and happily devouring it as though nothing had happened. Your drives to the lane might resemble a suburban dad riding his daughter's tricycle, all exaggerated angles and sudden lurching changes in direction and momentum and always just on the edge of collapse, and then you'd shoot off the wrong foot, maybe over the wrong shoulder. You did this less often as you got older, but it was still comforting that it existed within the realm of possibility. I wanted to remember that, not you saying goodbye.

When I landed in Frankfurt, I scrolled through my Twitter and Instagram feeds and saw that you had been able to crack time in your final game in Dallas, bringing out an older model of yourself for the occasion, only missing the golden beach-bum hair. I saw that you punctuated a throwback thirty-point night with your signature one-legged fadeaway, a silhouette as iconic as any other in NBA history, after Jerry West's NBA logo and Michael Jordan's splay-legged Jumpman and maybe even before Kareem Abdul-Jabbar mid-sky-hook. It was perfect. The only way to end it. I smiled.

I missed my son.

I thought of the nights when it was just the two of us watching you—the milestone games, yes, but mainly just the average Tuesdays, the second night of a back-to-back when there was nothing to play for but that didn't matter to you or us. I barely knew a Dallas without you in it, but Isaac didn't know one at all. I sat there, scrolling through my phone and I thought: Why didn't we commemorate this

occasion together? Maybe I had been a coward. Maybe I was scared I didn't know how to be a father without the guardrail of your reliable fadeaway jumper.

You probably know as well as anyone: transatlantic flights can fuck you up.

The moment—and it was just a moment, a flicker—passed. No, basketball wouldn't end for us. No, the bond that it formed wouldn't dissolve. No, your part in that wouldn't disappear just because you weren't on the court anymore. No, you wouldn't be replaced by Luka Dončić or anyone else, no matter how we grew to love them, too. You couldn't be.

We see you, Big German. We'll always see you.

ACKNOWLEDGMENTS

I could win the lottery every week for a year and still the best thing that will ever happen to me is that I am the father of Isaac Crain. He is the heart and soul of this book, even if he doesn't show up until halfway through. Just consider it an extremely long introduction.

Other than Isaac (and, of course, Dirk himself), Will Evans is the main reason this book exists. I had considered writing about Dirk a couple of times over the years, but I was never able to come up with an idea beyond "Dirk book???" until he asked me in the summer of 2019 if I would be interested in giving this a shot. I think the general conceit of *I See You, Big German* (and certainly the title) came to me during that first conversation. When Will told me he wanted it to be personal, my mind immediately snapped to one book in particular: Hanif Abdurraqib's *Go Ahead In the Rain*. Hanif did not invent the open letter format, but his ode to A Tribe Called Quest (also a formative influence on me) is absolutely what I was thinking of when I conceived this project. I call this a "memoir about Dirk Nowitzki," and Hanif's example helped me get there.

Bob Mehr—in addition to being a dear, trusted friend for

a couple of decades now, and a much better writer than me—was invaluable as an early reader. Bob would probably say he didn't do much, but, for once in the long time I've known him, he would be dead wrong. This book would be my 2006 NBA Finals without his assistance. If you enjoyed it, it's because Bob kept me from fucking it up.

I'm not sure if Stefania Morandi has ever seen a full NBA game, or even most of one, but I did not need her for that. She was absolutely clutch in keeping me motivated and encouraged throughout the writing process. It would be difficult to overstate her importance in keeping me pressing forward, especially when my hand was killing me because I had decided to write the entire first draft of this long-hand in a series of notebooks that were about the size of an iPhone 3. (Speaking of, shout out to Walgreens and their Wexford Mini Composition Books.)

A big thank you goes to the members of the Mavericks organization past and present who talked to me for (or helped me facilitate) various pieces over the years, which served as the bones for this book: Mark Cuban, Donnie Nelson, Rick Carlisle, Scott Tomlin, Sarah Melton, Casey Smith, Jason Terry, Shawn Marion, Tyson Chandler, Steve Nash, Al Whitley, J.J. Barea, Jason Kidd, Roddy Beaubois, Cedric Ceballos, Lisa Tyner, Mark Followill, Jeff "Skin" Wade, Brian Dameris, Brian Cardinal, Zaza Pachulia, Darrell Armstrong, Devin Harris, Dwight Powell, and Maxi Kleber. Also, thank you to the legends Marc Stein, Holger Geschwindner, and Charles Barkley for their contributions.

Others who deserve recognition, and much more than just a few words here: Nikki Rosen (for giving me Isaac and also convincing us to get half-season tickets, even if we could barely afford them), my mom and dad and sister and brother, Josh Venable (who has been with me for all of this and more), my *D Magazine* fam, and anyone who ever tried to punch me during a basketball game (I forgive you, it only made me stronger). See you in twenty years for the follow-up: *My Slovenian Son: Luka Dončić* and *What He Means to Dallas (and Me)*.

La Reunion

La Reunion Publishing is an imprint of Deep Vellum established in 2019 to share the stories of the people and places of Texas. La Reunion is named after the utopian socialist colony founded by Frenchman Victor Considerant on the west bank of the Trinity River across from the then-fledgling town of Dallas in 1855. Considerant considered Texas as the promised land: a land of unbridled and unparalleled opportunity, with its story yet to be written, and the La Reunion settlers added an international mindset and pioneering spirit that is still reflected in Dallas, and across Texas, today. La Reunion publishes books that explore the story of Texas from all sides, critically engaging with the myths, histories, and the untold stories that make Texas the land of literature come to life.